D0747056

LIFE, LOVE, FAITH, FAMILY
Perspectives from a Veteran Church Leader

Gerald B. Kieschnick

CONCORDIA PUBLISHING HOUSE · SAINT LOUIS

Published by Concordia Publishing House
3558 S. Jefferson Ave., St. Louis, MO 63118-3968
1-800-325-3040 • cph.org

Manufactured in the United States of America

1 2 3 4 5 6 7 8 9 10   27 26 25 24 23 22 21 20 19 18

CONTENTS

This book is dedicated to my sainted father, Martin; my 102-year-old mother, Elda; my wife, Terry; our daughter, Angie; our son, Andrew; our son-in-law, Todd; our grandson, Kolby; and our granddaughter, Kayla. Along with grandparents, siblings, and other close relatives, these are the people who have filled my life with love, the family with whom I share life-giving faith in our Lord and Savior Jesus Christ.

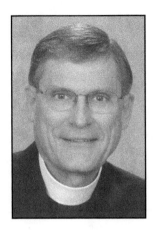

Preface

For more than half a century, I've served in numerous Christian leadership capacities, from developing a mission church starting with nothing to president of a national church body of over two million members. Throughout those years, I've met and known many people who experience much joy, meaning, and fulfillment in life and love. Yet, many of these wonderful people have encountered challenges and difficulties along the way, often in the arenas of family and faith. Every week, for the past nine years, I've written my personal perspectives on these and a variety of other topics. In this little book, I share one hundred of those stories and reflections for your reading enjoyment, emotional encouragement, and spiritual enrichment.

Jerry Kieschnick

1

Father

VOLUME I, NUMBER 2—OCTOBER 22, 2009

January 1, 1983, was a very difficult day for our family. Marking the beginning of a new year of life for many, it also signaled the end of life on earth for my father. Martin Herbert Otto Kieschnick had battled for more than a year a cancerous tumor on his rib cage that just wouldn't go away. Surgery, hypothermal therapy, radiation, and every other remedy known to the medical world twenty-six years ago were unsuccessful. He slowly but steadily entered a fetal position and died. So on a day of celebration for most, it was a day of quiet grief for my father's wife, children, and grandchildren. We grieved because we had lost a very important man in our lives. We grieved quietly because we all had come to realize that this man of much strength was becoming weaker by the day, losing his struggle for life. Accordingly, we had begun to pray that God would be gracious and end Martin's suffering. That prayer was answered on New Year's Day.

The visitation at the funeral home the next day was tough. The reality and power of death was taking its toll. Emotions flowed freely—sadness at the loss of a man who had meant so much to so many; thanksgiving for his freedom from pain and suffering; inexplicable anger that momentarily and uncharacteristically prompted me to want to hit a door or a wall; emptiness at realizing the happy and safe times we spent together with Dad in charge would never be the same; joy that through God's grace by faith in Christ, Martin was in the eternal presence of God. In addition, the new but very real awareness arose within me that a virtual layer of insulation between me and eternity had been removed. I realized that, generationally speaking, in the journey of life I was now next in line before the threshold of death. Dad has been in my thoughts and remembrances every day since that day in January. On many of those days, I've recalled words of life like these: "Grandchildren are the crown of the aged, and the glory of children is their fathers" (Proverbs 17:6).

2

The Price of Freedom

VOLUME I, NUMBER 5—NOVEMBER 12, 2009

Veterans Day was observed this week. Men and women of our armed forces have made many sacrifices to preserve and defend the freedoms we Americans enjoy. Parents leave children behind. Children leave parents behind. Married military men and women leave spouses behind. Some, making the ultimate sacrifice of life itself, do not return home alive. And some even die before leaving. How tragic it was to see and hear the recent reports from Fort Hood, Texas. One obviously deranged soldier killed thirteen people and injured twenty-eight others, some of whom might not survive. What could have prompted such outrageous action? Why did so many have to die? Some may even ask, "Where is God?" when these tragedies occur.

Such heart-wrenching queries remind us of the broken and fallen world in which we live, where evil still has its day as "the devil prowls around like a roaring lion, seeking someone to devour" (1 Peter 5:8). The only answer to these questions that makes sense is the life-giving message of the Bible, which tells us that our Savior, Jesus Christ, has destroyed the power of sin, death, and the devil. He alone offers the comfort and healing that can fill the emptiness of lives left vacant by the sadness and sorrow in the tragic deaths of soldiers, family members, and friends. In even the most terrible of circumstances, we have hope. For God is there, "in Christ . . . reconciling the world to Himself" (2 Corinthians 5:19).

3

A Special Christmas Gift

VOLUME I, NUMBER 11—DECEMBER 24, 2009

Quite a few years ago, my wife, Terry, suggested that I make a dollhouse for our seven-year-old daughter's Christmas present. I agreed. We drove our station wagon to the lumber store, purchased the necessary material, and headed home. Child restraints and seat belts were not what they are today, so Angie sat in the back of the vehicle on the small stack of lumber that would soon become her dollhouse.

As we drove home, she asked, "Daddy, what are you going to build with this lumber?" While I don't clearly recall the answer I gave, I suspect my response was not exactly the whole truth and nothing but the truth. There was no way I was going to spoil the surprise Terry had in mind. To keep the surprise a secret, I confined my work on the project to the garage after bedtime hours. On Christmas Eve, Angie was totally surprised and thrilled. Terry was happy. The dollhouse hasn't fallen apart after all these years. It was a special Christmas gift!

The great thrill that special gift brought into my daughter's life many years ago does not even come close to comparing with the thrill I receive every year at Christmas in the celebration of God's gift—Jesus, the holy child born in Bethlehem's manger. Having been long foretold, His birth was neither a secret nor a surprise. Heralded by angels to humble shepherds, sought out and worshiped by kings from afar, worshiped by people around the world after all these years, this King of kings and Lord of lords is the most special gift ever given!

4

An Inning to Remember

Volume I, Number 23—March 11, 2010

In the first game of a doubleheader high school base-ball tournament in Texas, the team I was support-ing managed to turn a 5-0 lead into a 12-5 loss. The pitchers had poor control that day, yielding quite a few unearned runs. Our pitchers struggled again in the second game, providing free trips to first base and beyond, with unhappy results on the scoreboard. Some wild pitches bounced in the dirt, a couple of them hit the batter, and some got past the catcher, generously allowing runners to score. Finally, the coach called the second baseman to the pitcher's mound. This young man—a sophomore playing with the varsity team—had pitched earlier in his career. But he had not yet pitched in a high school game, playing instead at second or third base.

He took over the mound in the bottom of the fourth inning, his team behind 5-2. There were no outs. The bases were loaded. Some in the stands were won-dering what the coach was thinking. But calmly and coolly, the young pitcher struck out the first batter, much to the home team crowd's surprise and delight! The second batter grounded out to the shortstop. And then, in a breathtaking moment, the third batter also struck out, frozen by a wicked curveball! The crowd went wild! Although our team's offense was unproductive, resulting in the second loss of the day, this new young pitcher provided his team, his coaches, and his fans with an inning to remember. Oh, and did I mention that the pitcher's name is Kolby and that he's my grandson?

Have a great day!

And remember that the talents God gives us are not always obvious until we're called upon to use them in difficult times under what may appear to be hopeless circumstances.

[Oh, by the way, the next day our team was trailing 6-1 in the bottom half of the last inning. After the team narrowed the score to 6-5, a batter drove in the tying run and scored the winning run while there were two outs! Guess who that was! *Two* innings and *two* games to remember!]

5

Enduring Hardship . . . in God's Hands

VOLUME I, NUMBER 26—APRIL 1, 2010

I recently read fascinating books offering hope and encouragement and stories that inspire and uplift. One I started this week is titled *Shores of Hope*. It tells the story of the emigration of some of my ancestors, a Slavonic group called Wends from eastern Germany. Over a period of years, they left their homes between Berlin and Dresden, mostly for economic and religious reasons. They sailed to Australia, the United States, Canada, South America, and South Africa. My group landed in Galveston, Texas, in 1854.

One passenger describes the hardships of a trip that took from four to six months. "I can't describe the enormity of the danger at sea. . . . The waves were very high and the ship was rocking back and forth."[1] He goes on to describe conditions on board, including seasickness, diarrhea, epidemics, poor food, spoiled water, miserably close sleeping quarters, dirt, litter, fleas, lice, bedbugs, varmints, wretched stench, gossip, quarreling, philandering (the latter three surely not descriptive of the activities of any Lutheran travelers), and frequent infant deaths at sea. Upon departure, one said prophetically, "With fearful hearts, standing on the ship and thinking that everything might perish, we commended ourselves totally into God's hands."[2] Although our lives today are fraught with challenges, most of them pale in comparison to those faced by our forefathers in life and in faith. Following their lead, we also endure the hardships we face, knowing that we are always in God's hands!

---

1   Trudla Malinkowa, *Shores of Hope: Wends Go Overseas* (Austin, TX: Concordia University Press, 2009), n.p.
2   Malinkowa, *Shores of Hope*, n.p.

Bad News/Good News

VOLUME I, NUMBER 29—APRIL 22, 2010

The bad news is that last week our son-in-law's pickup truck was stolen. It's a Ford F-250 quad cab diesel—the truck of his dreams. Although it is nine years old, paid for, and well used, it's like a member of the family. So when Todd came out of the Home Depot and saw an empty space where his truck was parked only minutes earlier, he was crushed. The police investigator said this model is a favorite of truck thieves. He also said it probably would be used to make a quick trip across the US-Mexico border, returning with undocumented workers who are willing to pay a thousand dollars per person for the privilege of a seven-hour ride, crammed in the space where the back seat once was, in order to find well-waged work here in the US.

The good news is that two days later, our daughter, Angie, called and said, "They found Todd's truck!" It was in one piece; but it was full of beer cans, soda cans, and cigarette butts, and the back seat had been removed. The taillights were damaged, not by the villains, but by the tow truck that had transported the vehicle from its discovery location, with eleven other stolen trucks, to the city police pound in a small-town pasture twenty miles east of Austin. It needed a new starter and a thorough cleaning, but it has been returned to a very happy owner. I shared that good news with my staff, together with Jesus' parable of the lost (and later found) coin, which ends with these words: "And when she has found it, she calls together her friends and neighbors, saying, 'Rejoice with me, for I have found the coin that I had lost.' Just so, I tell you, there is joy before the angels of God over one sinner who repents" (Luke 15:9–10).

Discerning and Understanding the Will of God

Volume I, Number 43—July 29, 2010

For many years, I've wrestled with discerning the will of God and trying to understand it. I'm not alone. That's the lot of every human being. Old and New Testament characters faced this dilemma—Moses, Abraham, Joseph, Joshua, Elisha, David, Solomon, Job, Elizabeth and Zechariah, Mary and Joseph, the twelve disciples of Jesus, the apostle Paul, and many others. To some, God made His will known through a dream or an angel. To others, the Lord Himself spoke directly. And to still others, God revealed His will through events and experiences. God's will in my life has not always been readily, unmistakably, or clearly revealed. No direct revelation has come my way. Instead, prayerful reflection, careful evaluation, thoughtful collaboration, painful cogitation, and intense spiritual deliberation have been part of the process of discerning God's will for my life, both prior to and throughout my forty years of ministry.

For example, an academic failure in my collegiate years eventually led to a change of vocational calling from veterinary medicine to pastoral ministry. At the time that failure occurred, I questioned God's will and for some time had no clue what it might be. But through that experience I met the wonderful young lady who has now been my wife for forty-four and a half years. I soon understood why that setback occurred and discerned God's will as a result. In all struggles in life, I always recall God's message to His people exiled in Babylon: "For I know the plans I have for you, declares the LORD, plans for welfare and not for evil, to give you a future and a hope" (Jeremiah 29:11). Those words provide help and hope for me in discerning and understanding the will of God. I pray they will provide the same for you and for all in our beloved Synod.

8

Escalating Tension

VOLUME II, NUMBER 3—SEPTEMBER 16, 2010

One would need to have lived in a cave the past several years not to be aware of escalating tension in America and around the world. That particularly came to mind this past week on the ninth anniversary of the death and destruction in New York, Washington, and Pennsylvania at the hands of terrorists on September 11, 2001. It was further heightened by widespread news reports that the pastor of Dove World Outreach Center in Gainesville, Florida, was planning to burn thousands of copies of the Qur'an, the Muslim holy book. With the ongoing conflict in the Middle East, continued recession, troublesome rates of unemployment and stock market fluctuation, it's easy to understand the escalating tension in our country and world today.

Different people respond to tension in different ways. Some choose alcohol, drugs (prescription and nonprescription), pornography, and other abusive or addictive behavior in an effort to seek relief, even if only temporary, from stress, pressure, and pain. Others deal with tension through involvement in politics, hobbies, or various avocations. Still others rely trustingly on the words of Jesus in Matthew 6: "Do not be anxious about your life, what you will eat or what you will drink, nor about your body, what you will put on. Is not life more than food, and the body more than clothing? . . . Your heavenly Father knows that you need them all. But seek first the kingdom of God and His righteousness, and all these things will be added to you" (vv. 25, 32–33).

The hymnist writes:

Oh, for a faith that will not shrink
Tho' pressed by many a foe;
That will not tremble on the brink
Of poverty or woe.

A faith that shines more bright and clear
When tempests rage without;
That, when in danger, knows no fear,
In darkness feels no doubt.

Lord, give us such a faith as this;
And then, whate'er may come,
We'll taste e'en now the hallowed bliss
Of an eternal home.

—"Oh, for a Faith That Will Not Shrink" (*TLH* 396:1, 3, 6)

Unanswered Prayers

Volume II, Number 5—September 30, 2010

Some years ago, Garth Books sang about "Unanswered Prayers." In the song, he wondered whether or not unanswered prayers meant that God wasn't listening, or just maybe, the prayers were truly answered in ways we can't understand. There are days when the words of that song are a helpful reminder of providential protection and provision, even when such do not appear to be forthcoming from the God to whom belongs all power and might. While we believe God answers all the prayers of His faithful people, we know that sometimes His answers are not what we'd like them to be. Even when God does not answer prayers the way we'd like, He still loves, cares for, and knows what's best for His children. That's a difficult truth to remember and sometimes even to believe.

I've prayed often for specific signs of God's presence in my life. Some of those prayers are answered almost before the "Amen" is spoken. I'm still waiting for other prayers to be answered. In fact, I'm praying very fervently right now for God's provision in a certain way. I'm not a patient man to begin with, particularly when God's timing and mine do not appear to be in sync. The difficulty is in knowing that God is at work in my life, even when my prayers seem to go unanswered. This experience is neither unique nor uncommon. I imagine it is shared right now by some of the folks reading these words. I pray for men and women like you, who know what it means when God obviously answers our prayers. I also pray for folks who wait for God's sign that what appear to be ungranted petitions are in fact not unanswered prayers.

Reformation and Reform

VOLUME II, NUMBER 10—NOVEMBER 4, 2010

We in the Protestant segment of the Body of Christ just completed our celebration of the 493rd anniversary of the Reformation. For many, this event is more than significant. For many others, October 31 is no more and no less than Halloween. The former tend to be a bit academic in observing this radical, personally hazardous, world-changing phenomenon. The latter welcome an excuse, though they mostly find it not at all necessary to have one, for raucous revelry and irreverent imbibing.

The Protestant Reformation inaugurated by God in the sixteenth centuries aimed to restore the pure proclamation of the Gospel in the Church, which had become covered over and distorted through the course of centuries by false doctrine and false practice. This Reformation brought about the rediscovery of the good news of Jesus Christ, endorsing with ringing clarity the great biblical principles of *sola gratia, sola fide, sola scriptura*. The need for reformation is constant in the Church. What needs to be reformed? Certainly not the church's message: Jesus Christ came to save the world. And certainly not the mission: to make known the love of Christ to as many people as possible. Rather, we need always to be renewed in our sense of concern for the eternal destiny of people, and a spirit of boldness and commitment to do something with that concern! The people of God are compelled to a reformation of spirit, propelling us into action in Christ's kingdom. True reformation demands and produces genuine reform. *O Lord, reform the Church. Begin with me!*

A Blessed Christmas!

VOLUME II, NUMBER 17—DECEMBER 23, 2010

Two days before Christmas, many Americans and others throughout the world are focused on preparation for the celebration of the birth of our Lord Jesus Christ. The real reason for the season may not be known by or occur to many such preparers, namely those who see Christmas as merely a holiday when many offices are closed and services interrupted. But those of us who know what this day is really all about have our hearts and minds, at least partially, tuned in to the significance of this very important day.

Our new home has been blessed by Christmas cards and letters we've received from around the country, each with special greetings from very special people. Two had particularly memorable messages:

God spoke . . . and the world began.
God heard . . . and promised a Savior.
God loved . . . and came to dwell among us.

Jesus is

– the Lamb of God, to die for our sins.
– the Prince of Peace, to change our hearts.
– the Good Shepherd, to guide our lives.

Terry and I pray for each of you at this meaningful time of year a special measure of the peace of God that passes all understanding, a very merry and most richly blessed Christmas!

Happy New Year!

VOLUME II, NUMBER 18—DECEMBER 30, 2010

Today is almost the last day of the last year of the first decade of the twenty-first century. The revolution of the calendar to a new year brings reflections of the past year and, in this case, the past decade. News reports this week have recalled the people, places, problems, and perplexities of the past ten years, especially 2010. Many families recall loved ones and friends who have gone ahead of them into heaven. My family is one of those, observing the twenty-eighth anniversary of my father's passing on New Year's Day in 1983. Such remembrances bring to mind the reality that life on earth is brief, temporary, and not without its joys and sorrows, victories and defeats, difficulties and blessings. In a sinful world, we do our best to live life to its fullest, knowing that, as a friend recently reminded me, Jesus did not come into a perfect world.

New Year's Day is also a catalyst for many people to make resolutions. Some resolutions are actually new. Others are preowned or recycled. In most cases, New Year's resolutions are well-intentioned expressions of hopes and dreams that may or may not ever become reality. Their ultimate fate depends on numerous circumstances, some in and some out of the resolver's control. In that regard, I share with you a quote I found several years ago from Admiral Jim Stockdale, a POW at the "Hanoi Hilton" from 1965–1973: "You must never confuse faith that you will prevail in the end—which you can never afford to lose—with the discipline to confront the most brutal facts of your current reality, whatever they might be."

Whatever "the most brutal facts of your current reality" might be, Terry and I express to you our hopes and prayers that yours might be indeed a happy, meaningful, and fulfilling New Year, under the blessing and grace of God!

13

They Invited Jesus to the Wedding

VOLUME II, NUMBER 22—JANUARY 27, 2011

Saturday, January 29, 1966, was a cold winter day on which Terry and I exchanged our vows of faithfulness to each other before the altar of the Lord at St. Paul Lutheran Church in Austin, Texas. The night before was our wedding rehearsal and rehearsal dinner. I had driven the hundred miles from Texas A&M in College Station to the rehearsal. After dinner with the wedding party and family members, I kissed Terry goodbye at midnight and drove back, getting to bed around 2:30 a.m. Four and a half hours later, at 7:00 a.m., I was taking a graduate biochemistry course final exam, after which I returned to Austin for the wedding. That day was also my twenty-third birthday, which has made our anniversary a fairly easy date to remember. That night the thermometer dropped to 12 degrees in Salado, the historic site of our two-day honeymoon.

The text for the sermon at our wedding was John 2:2: "Jesus also was invited to the wedding with His disciples." It describes the first miracle of Jesus, turning water into wine at the wedding in Cana of Galilee. Pastor Albert Jesse encouraged us to remember that Jesus was a very real part of our wedding that night and would be with us throughout our lifetime together. While we, like most couples, have had moments of struggle, tension, and disagreement, my father's comment before the wedding was right: "This marriage was made in heaven." Jesus has been and continues to be the most important part of our lives together. I thank God for my dear wife and the self-giving love she has freely and sacrificially shared with me, our children, grandchildren, and other family members, and with many, many people in our country and around the world. Happy anniversary, sweetheart! I love you with all my heart!

14

Cars in the Garage

VOLUME II, NUMBER 23—FEBRUARY 3, 2011

Our cars are in the garage! Isn't that where they belong? Indeed. During one of our recent moves we had an entire space designated as holding place for boxes of stuff awaiting attention. That attention having been sufficiently given, enough space was cleared two weeks ago to accommodate our two cars. Mind you, there's not an abundance of space left over. As a matter of fact, my car, a 2004 Buick, has an overall length of 206.8 inches. With its nose touching the workbench in front, a mere 2.4 inches of space remains between the rear bumper and the garage door. It's a close fit! Terry's car is 11.3 inches shorter than mine, resulting in a much more comfortable fit. I suppose this means one important fact to consider for my next automobile purchase is overall length.

This experience has been an exercise in thanksgiving to God for blessings received. The stuff in the boxes, while representing a challenge with which to deal, is tangible evidence of precious possessions procured with the proceeds of hard work and careful purchases. Actually, some of those possessions are only semi-precious, but they surely must have seemed precious at the time of purchase. In the process of packing and moving, we've rediscovered what we've known all our lives—possessions are not nearly as precious as people. So while we've successfully parked our cars in the garage—an achievement for which I'm very thankful—I'm much more thankful for the people who ride in our cars and yours as well. So drive safely, and no texting!

Hedonism and the Grammy Awards

VOLUME II, NUMBER 25—FEBRUARY 17, 2011

Perhaps it's just chronological maturation, but it seems to me that America is growing more hedonistic by the day. Last Sunday Terry and I attended the installation of a pastor friend of mine in San Antonio and stopped in New Braunfels for dinner with my almost-ninety-five-year-old mother, Elda. Mind you, there's nothing hedonistic about either of those events. However, after we got home around 9:00 p.m., I sat down to read the Sunday newspaper, turned on the TV, and saw that the Grammy Awards were still on. With one eye on the paper and the other on the screen, I saw in the last hour of the three-and-a-half-hour production enough stuff to make me somewhere between disgusted and repulsed.

Some of the singers and dancers were good and actually even entertaining. Sadly, others sang or rapped words that were deemed inappropriate enough by those responsible for such things to be muted during the actual presentation. More than one performer placed his or her hand on his or her crotch. Others engaged in gyrations that in most civilized cultures would be relegated to intimate marital privacy rather than a public stage and vast television audience.

According to a thesaurus, synonyms for *hedonistic* are "self-indulgent, riotous, wild, pleasure-seeking, and self-gratifying." While I can't vouch for the first two hours of the Grammy Awards, those words seem like a fairly accurate description of the last third of the program. "The works of the flesh are evident: sexual immorality, impurity, sensuality, . . . drunkenness, orgies, and things like these. I warn you, as I warned you before, that those who do such things will not inherit the kingdom of God" (Galatians 5:19, 21). Those are important words for America to consider.

Living Christian Values

VOLUME II, NUMBER 31—MARCH 31, 2011

For the past several months I've initiated conversations with people of many kinds—lay, clergy, male, female, young, and not-so-young—probing the question of how we in the Christian faith, particularly in The Lutheran Church—Missouri Synod, view and live our lives in accordance with Christian values. Interestingly, much of that conversation has focused on identifying those values. Examples include but are not limited to faith, life, health, family, forgiveness, freedoms, faithfulness, honesty, integrity, service, stewardship, self-discipline, leadership, relationships, and vocational calling. In addition to identifying such values, an important part of the conversation has been defining them in simple, understandable, communicable, meaningful terms.

While past Perspectives articles have been neither serial nor sequential, I plan at least temporarily to interrupt my historic system of seemingly serendipitous selection of topics for these weekly epistles and will devote the next several Perspectives articles to some or all of the Christian values listed above. If or when special circumstances or unplanned events occur, it may be necessary or prudent to interrupt this series. Thanks for your understanding. That caveat expressed, I do look forward to what could be a stretch, namely, addressing very important topics succinctly, pointedly, theologically, practically, and adequately. Not a simple task for one who is both blessed and challenged with some of that DNA referenced above. Nevertheless, I pray this series will be a blessing to anyone who, like yours truly, cherishes Christian values and is daily challenged by the devil, the world, and my own sinful flesh in living them.

Living Christian Values—Faith

VOLUME II, NUMBER 32—APRIL 7, 2011

For this first in a series on Living Christian Values, I've chosen to begin with faith, defined as "confidence, trust, reliance, assurance, conviction, belief, loyalty, commitment, dedication." Biblical definitions and references abound. Hebrews says, "Faith is the assurance of things hoped for, the conviction of things not seen" (11:1), and describes Abel, Enoch, Noah, Abraham, Sarah, Isaac, Jacob, Joseph, Moses, and Rahab as Old Testament people of faith.

In the New Testament, examples of men and women of faith abound, including (on good days) the disciples of Jesus. Also noted are the apostles, along with Timothy, Titus, Stephen, Phoebe, Priscilla, Aquila, and many others. St. Paul writes that we are "justified by faith apart from works of the law" (Romans 3:28), that "since we have been justified by faith, we have peace with God through our Lord Jesus Christ" (Romans 5:1), that "by grace you have been saved through faith" (Ephesians 2:8), and that "I live by faith in the Son of God, who loved me and gave Himself for me" (Galatians 2:20). Jesus said, "Everyone who lives and believes in Me shall never die" (John 11:26).

During a storm, Jesus called His disciples men "of little faith" (Matthew 8:26). Yet, when He saw the faith of the friends of a paralytic, Jesus healed the man and forgave his sins. He did the same for many others who had faith that He could help, heal, restore, save, or resurrect them. He healed the blind, the deaf, the lame, the possessed. He declared, "Whatever you ask in prayer, you will receive, if you have faith" (Matthew 21:22). Sometimes those words seem far away, especially when prayers are not answered in the way we think they should be. Yet, what a blessing it is that we receive faith as a free gift of God's grace through Holy Baptism and that our faith is nurtured and strengthened through Holy Communion. Faith in God's omniscient and gracious providence makes it possible to live with hope and security in a world that is wrecked, racked, and ruined by sin. While my faith often appears dimmer than I'd like in the face of biblical examples and other powerful testimonies, I am bold to pray: "Lord I believe. Help me in moments of doubt and uncertainty." Faith—a living Christian value!

18

Living Christian Values—Life

VOLUME II, NUMBER 33—APRIL 14, 2011

Life is a great mystery. To me, that is most obvious at the time of death. One moment a person is warm, communicative, and usually at least somewhat capable of movement. The next moment that same person is cold, silent, and still. The word *lifeless* is aptly descriptive. Our daughter nailed it when as a three-year-old she asked, "Daddy, when a person dies, does he take off his body?" That was quite perceptive, especially for such a young lady. When a person dies as a believer in Christ, Christians believe that person's spirit or soul goes to heaven and leaves behind the body that has been inhabited by the spirit or soul throughout that person's life. The mystery of life is both more easily understood and much more complicated when viewed from the perspective of the reality of death. Death is so final and takes from loved ones the life and presence of the person who died. That's why life is a very important, even vital, Christian value.

While not everyone agrees, it's obvious to me and to many that life begins at conception and ends at death. The Supreme Court's 1973 *Roe v. Wade* decision legalized abortion in the United States, declaring that viability (the ability of a fetus to live outside the womb) usually occurs between the twenty-fourth and twenty-eighth week of pregnancy, as if the living being inside the womb before that time does not exist. Wikipedia says that "*Roe v. Wade* reshaped national politics, dividing much of the nation into pro-choice and pro-life camps, while activating grassroots movements on both sides."[3] It has been estimated that more than fifty million abortions have occurred since *Roe v. Wade*. Notwithstanding that sad and grievous reality, legislatures in thirty states are considering or passing bills that would restrict abortion rights, ban most abortions twenty weeks after conception, and block public or private insurance coverage for abortions. While that's a step in the right direction, much work remains before respect for and protection of human life fully demonstrates what the God-given gift of life, from the womb to the tomb, really is—a living Christian value!

---

3   https://en.wikipedia.org/wiki/Roe_v._Wade, accessed July 6, 2018.

Living Christian Values—The Empty Tomb

VOLUME II, NUMBER 34—APRIL 21, 2011

It may seem surprising to some that I would choose the empty tomb as a living Christian value. Actually, it seems quite appropriate to me. This article is written during Holy Week, which signals the culmination of Lent. Maundy Thursday is the birthday of the Lord's Supper. Good Friday is the day of the crucifixion and burial of Jesus. Holy Saturday commemorates the day that the body of Jesus lay in the tomb. Easter Sunday is the Festival of the Resurrection of our Lord. It's difficult for the human mind to imagine that a person who was clearly dead and buried in a tomb sealed with a large stone could in fact come back to life, miraculously make his exit from that tomb, and be seen alive, in bodily form, by hundreds of people in the next forty days. For centuries since that time, secular and religious scholars have sought either to disprove or to confirm the truth of the empty tomb. Many who at first sought to disprove that truth eventually ended up confirming it.

Simon Greenleaf, one of the principal founders of the Harvard Law School, originally set out to disprove the biblical testimony concerning the resurrection of Jesus. He believed that a careful examination of the internal witness of the Gospels would dispel all the myths at the heart of Christianity. But this legal scholar came to the conclusion that the witnesses were reliable, and that the resurrection did in fact happen. St. Paul says it well: "If there is no resurrection of the dead, then not even Christ has been raised. . . . And if Christ has not been raised, your faith is futile and you are still in your sins. . . . But in fact Christ has been raised from the dead. . . . For as in Adam all die, so also in Christ shall all be made alive" (1 Corinthians 15:13, 17, 20, 22). Martin Luther wrote, "He [Jesus] rises again from the dead, in order by His resurrection to pave the way to eternal life for us, and to aid us against eternal death."[4] The resurrection of Christ is critical to the Christian faith. Someday all who die in Christ will live again. The empty tomb—a living Christian value!

---

4   *Concordia Triglotta*, "Statements Made by Luther in 1531 and 1533," ed. Friedrich Bente (St. Louis: Concordia Publishing House, 1921), section 248, p. 222.

Living Christian Values—Marriage

VOLUME II, NUMBER 35—APRIL 28, 2011

The big news this week besides burdensomely high (and steadily rising) gasoline prices in the United States is the marriage of Great Britain's Prince William to Kate Middleton. Scheduled for Friday, April 29, at 11:00 a.m. London time (2:00 a.m. CDT), the wedding is predicted to be viewed by two billion people worldwide. Live commentary will be provided by Diane Sawyer, Barbara Walters, Gretchen Carlson, and a host of other notables. While many other weddings will occur that same weekend around the world, none will receive anywhere near the notoriety of the royal nuptials mentioned above. And in all likelihood, none will come even close to the horrendous expense of that wedding, mostly paid for by someone other than the royal couple. Nevertheless, whether royalty or not, this weekend's festivities bring worldwide attention to the rite of marriage, blessed by God himself when he made the first man and the first woman.

In my generation, it was widely assumed that the wedding vows spoken by a bride and groom (usually at a Christian altar) would indeed be a lifelong commitment, and for many it still is. I thank God that Terry and I have been married forty-five years! Today, it is estimated that nearly 50 percent of all first marriages, over 60 percent of second marriages, and more than 70 percent of third marriages end in divorce. Children of divorced parents often experience difficult emotions and bear many scars for the rest of their lives. Conversely, blessings abound when husband and wife fulfill their pledge of faithfulness: "I take you to be my wedded (wife/husband), to have and to hold from this day forward, for better, for worse, for richer, for poorer, in sickness and in health, to love and to honor and to cherish, till death parts us, according to God's Holy Word; I pledge to you my love and faithfulness." The writer of Genesis said, "Therefore a man shall leave his father and his mother and hold fast to his wife, and they shall become one flesh" (Genesis 2:24). Thank God for marriage—a living Christian value!

Living Christian Values—Freedom

VOLUME II, NUMBER 36—MAY 5, 2011

Late this past Sunday night, regular TV programming was interrupted by newscasters announcing that a special statement would be forthcoming from the President of the United States. President Obama announced that in a special operation in Abbottabad, Pakistan, United States military forces had killed Osama bin Laden. The long-hunted al-Qaeda leader and chief architect of the deadliest terrorist attack on US soil on September 11, 2001, was subsequently buried at sea. News programs Monday morning were devoted largely if not entirely to details of the story of bin Laden's death, providing at least temporary respite from the tragic news of death and destruction from tornadoes that struck much of the southeastern part of our country the week before. We certainly hold in our prayers all who lost loved ones, homes, and possessions in those horrendous storms, even as we have done the same for almost a decade for those most directly and dramatically affected by the events of 9/11.

After the bin Laden news had spread, near euphoric celebrations occurred throughout many parts of our land. His death brought a sense that, at least in one important way, justice had been carried out. It also provided opportunity for release of many emotions carried in the hearts of Americans and others around the world who have witnessed from afar or been personally affected by multiple suicide bombings and other atrocities perpetrated by Islamic terrorists. This event also provided demonstrable expression of the value we place on freedom, certainly in America, and also throughout the world. The recent overthrows of dictatorships in Egypt, Tunisia, Uganda, Syria, Yemen, with more surely to come, are strong indications of the intrinsic value people inherently place on freedom. After living for decades or even centuries under dictatorial control, eventually people decide that freedom is worth the price it sometimes requires—death. "For freedom Christ has set us free" (Galatians 5:1). I thank God for a wonderful blessing we enjoy, defend, and celebrate: freedom—a living Christian value!

Living Christian Values—Family

Volume II, Number 37—May 12, 2011

The first family in recorded biblical history consisted of Adam and Eve and their sons Cain and Abel. All was not well between these two brothers. Eventually, Cain took Abel's life. Later, Adam and Eve were blessed with another son named Seth and had "other sons and daughters" (Genesis 5:4). We can only assume that these "other sons and daughters" married each other and that their multiple offspring were vital in the continuation of the human species God created with Adam and Eve. While no mention is made of how long Eve lived or whether Adam had other wives, we do know Adam was 930 years old when he died (Genesis 5:5). That first family experienced a mixture of peace and conflict in their life together. The same is true of almost all families since that time.

My family is wonderfully blessed with our mother, her four children, twelve grandchildren, and nineteen great-grandchildren. Including spouses, thirty-five of us gathered this past weekend to celebrate the ninety-fifth birthday of my mother, Elda. We are not without original sin, yet our time together was wonderfully peaceful and celebrative, thanking God for his many blessings. Many families enjoy similar blessings. Others do not. Over the same weekend when my family got together, in the middle of the night in our quiet central Texas town, a man shot and killed his estranged wife and her parents. In a crash following a high-speed police chase, he died instantly. Sadly, many families are broken. And while such violence is the exception, pain and suffering are not uncommon. Suffice it to say that the blessing of family, particularly where parents and children live together in love, mutual respect, spiritual vitality, and emotional health, is a wonderful gift of God! Indeed, a godly family is a living Christian value!

Living Christian Values—Self-Sacrifice

VOLUME II, NUMBER 38—MAY 19, 2011

Flooding this week continues from the Midwest to the Mississippi Delta. Army engineers opened the Morganza spillway, allowing the Mississippi River, swollen by snowmelt and heavy rains, to empty some of its excess baggage. This decision will hopefully head off flooding in the highly populated cities of Baton Rouge and New Orleans. It will also cause thousands of acres of farmland and as many as thirty thousand homes in the Atchafalaya River basin of Cajun country to flood. Those whose lives will be affected by this decision are in my prayers. I can only imagine how they feel toward the Corps of Engineers and the residents of the large cities, all of whom have direct or indirect connection to the loss of property and possessions about to occur.

In a very real way, whether voluntarily and happily or not, the evacuees are demonstrating a remarkable act of self-sacrifice. In a very real and painful way, they are sacrificing peace and possessions, stability and security, home and happiness in order that others will hopefully be spared from the flooding and may retain those blessings in their lives. In reply to my texted assurance of prayers for him and his people, Southern District President Kurt Schultz replied, "We are surrounded by hurricanes, tornados, oil, floods, and the gracious arms of Jesus!" Jesus, who understands more than any of us the meaning of self-sacrifice—a living Christian value!

Living Christian Values— Forgiveness

VOLUME II, NUMBER 40—JUNE 2, 2011

A few decades ago the movie *Love Story* had the line, "Love means you never have to say 'I'm sorry.'" My feelings about that song today are the same as they were back then. Perhaps the writer intended to communicate that when two people are in love, they will know each other well enough to feel a sense of regret when feelings have been hurt or relationships have been bruised, and therefore the words "I'm sorry" don't actually need to be spoken. In my experience, actually saying the words "I'm sorry" when offense has been given provides opportunity for the offender to express remorse for harmful or sinful words or deeds and for the offended to respond to such penitence with words of pardon and forgiveness by simply saying, "I forgive you." At other times, forgiveness begins with the offended.

Consider the story of a nine-year-old boy named Joshua who got a bicycle for Christmas and rode it every day. One day, the bike was gone from its usual place. Running to his front yard, Joshua saw a man loading it into his car. He shouted, but the man drove off. Joshua had a strong faith and told his dad he forgave the thief and wanted the thief to know he was forgiven. So the next day he dictated a message that his mother wrote on a large poster board. Joshua signed it, stapled it to a sawhorse, and put it in the front yard: "To the person who stole my bike: You really hurt my feelings when you took my bike. But I am a Christian and because Jesus forgave me, I FORGIVE YOU!!!" When Joshua's father left for work the next day, the sign was facedown in the yard. But at the end of the driveway, the bike was back. It had new handlebars, grips, and front fork assembly! Forgiveness—a living Christian value that works!

Living Christian Values—
Honesty and Integrity

VOLUME II, NUMBER 41—JUNE 8, 2011

In an otherwise relatively slow news week, we've been seeing, hearing, and reading about a certain congressman who has gotten himself into a heap of trouble. The first problem is his juvenile, sophomoric behavior of texting inappropriate messages. The second problem is his vehement denial of involvement in this activity, later reversed by his admission of guilt. Sadly, this is not an isolated episode of irresponsible and sinful behavior. Neither circumstance nor position in life can inoculate individuals against such imbalanced and satanic temptation. This illustration and many others, similar or dissimilar, highlight the importance of honesty and integrity as living Christian values.

Nothing more quickly (and usually irreversibly) decimates confidence placed in a person than immature, wrongful behavior that betrays the trust of spouse, family, friends, or constituents. This is particularly egregious when the perpetrator is in a position of public responsibility and accountability. Such behavior, while bad enough in itself, is exacerbated by not telling the truth about it, not asking for forgiveness, and not being willing to accept the consequences. Honesty means telling the truth, the whole truth, and nothing but the truth. Integrity means living a life defined by moral principles and ethical standards, where deeds do not conflict with words. Lord, help us by Your grace to live the Christian values of honesty and integrity!

Living Christian Values—Service and Vocational Calling

VOLUME II, NUMBER 42—JUNE 16, 2011

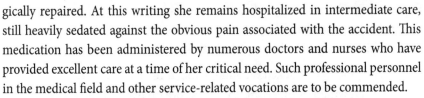

Some who read these articles are aware that this past Sunday night, the mother and brother of my dear wife, Terry, were in an auto accident in Austin. Her brother, David, is okay, but Dorothy, her mother, spent time in the ICU in critical condition with multiple fractures of the pelvis, eight ribs, and one scapula (that's a shoulder blade for the anatomically challenged). A badly broken wrist was surgically repaired. At this writing she remains hospitalized in intermediate care, still heavily sedated against the obvious pain associated with the accident. This medication has been administered by numerous doctors and nurses who have provided excellent care at a time of her critical need. Such professional personnel in the medical field and other service-related vocations are to be commended.

In addition to medical practitioners, I thank God often for public servants who provide police and fire protection, rescue and recovery, military defense, education, travel, lodging and food service, and a veritable host of other necessary services, whether or not directly related to matters of life and death. What a blessing that God has gifted each individual person with unique talents and abilities! And what a special blessing it is when those gifts are developed fully and utilized responsibly by people in service to mankind and in response to God's calling to vocational and professional endeavors! A country and western song by the band Alabama, after enumerating many service vocations, says it well: "Hello America! Let me thank you for your time!"

Living Christian Values— A Positive Outlook on Life

VOLUME II, NUMBER 43—JUNE 23, 2011

Some people see life as a glass that is half empty. Others see the glass as half full. After being named Commander of the Pacific Fleet by President Franklin Delano Roosevelt on December 7, 1941, Admiral Chester Nimitz assumed command on Christmas Eve of that year. While touring the destruction inflicted by the Japanese bombing of Pearl Harbor, he observed a spirit of despair, dejection, and defeat among the Americans. In reply to a question from one of his tour guides, Admiral Nimitz is reported to have said that the Japanese made three of the biggest mistakes an attack force could ever make. He then explained his statement:

1. The Japanese attacked on Sunday morning. Nine of every ten crewmen of those ships were ashore on leave. If the same ships had been lured to sea and then sunk, we would have lost 38,000 men instead of 3,800 men.

2. When the Japanese saw all those battleships lined in a row, they got so carried away sinking them that they never once bombed our dry docks opposite those ships. If they had destroyed the docks, we would have had to tow the ships to America to be repaired. As it is now, we can have them repaired and back at sea in the same amount of time we could have towed them to America.

3. Every drop of fuel in the Pacific theater of war is in top-of-the-ground storage tanks five miles away over that hill. One attack plane could have strafed those tanks and destroyed our fuel supply.

Times are tough! God is good! A positive outlook on life, such as the one personified by Admiral Nimitz, is a living Christian value!

Living Christian Values—Stewardship

Volume II, Number 44—June 30, 2011

As a young boy at home, I learned the art of financial stewardship from my father. Martin was a humble man whose intelligence and common sense took him way beyond what his high school education was designed to do. He supported our family as a meat cutter and eventually vice-president of a chain of food stores in Houston. Every Saturday night at home after work he opened the pay envelope containing the cash he had earned that week. He took a cigar box from his sock drawer and carefully placed exactly 10 percent of his pay into that box. That became the family offering the next day at St. Matthew Lutheran Church in Houston. He also added another amount that stayed in the box until the fall of each year. At that time the accumulated amount became the special mission festival offering for mission work in the nation and around the world.

Dad never instructed or scolded or warned or commanded me. He simply taught me the art of stewardship by his godly and joyful example. I've been blessed to share that joy with others throughout my ministry. In the mid-1970s as a young parish pastor, I recall a visitor to our congregation who happened to come to church one Sunday when I was preaching on the topic of stewardship. On the way out of church after the service, this visitor, looking perplexed, asked if he could take me to lunch the next week. During our meal, Bob pumped me about what I had said in the Sunday sermon about stewardship, a concept with which he was totally unfamiliar. Since that day he and his wife have become committed, faithful, joyful, and generous stewards of the significant blessings God has entrusted to their care. "Each one must give as he has decided in his heart, not reluctantly or under compulsion, for God loves a cheerful giver" (2 Corinthians 9:7).

Living Christian Values—Relationships

Volume II, Number 46—July 14, 2011

This past weekend, Terry and I attended a reunion of the descendants of my great-grandfather, Carl Otto Kieschnick. It was great to renew family relationships and to meet many of the 147 attendees who were unknown to us prior to this occasion. We thanked God for our ancestors, especially for my great-grandfather and great-grandmother, Carl and Christine Kieschnick, through whom our family became what it is today. Yes, there are such things as second cousins, once removed, and their name is legion! It was nearly one hundred years ago when Otto and Christine settled in Bishop, Texas, the once-robust town in which our reunion was held. Things have changed a lot since then. More about that next week. Suffice it to say that while we spent only a few hours together, the people who attended the reunion feel a stronger kinship with one another today than they did last week at this time.

That's true simply because relationships wilt when personal contact is absent, and they blossom when folks can see, communicate with, hug, cry with, and laugh with one another. The telling of stories about the past and present, coupled with sharing hopes and fears regarding the future, solidify existing relationships and provide solid foundation for new ones. Think of the relationships our ancestors formed when they left their homeland in eastern Germany and sailed across the Atlantic on a scarily small vessel for a new land, ending up in places like Galveston and Serbin, Texas. Like they, we also come to the realization about life expressed in 1 Chronicles 29:15: "We are here for only a moment, visitors and strangers in the land as our ancestors were before us. Our days on earth are like a passing shadow, gone so soon without a trace" (NLT). So we thank God for the time we have here on earth and for the relationships we form, particularly in the family of faith!

One Hundred Years Ago

VOLUME II, NUMBER 47—JULY 21, 2011

Last week I wrote about my family reunion, stating that nearly a hundred years ago my great-grandparents settled in a little town in south Texas that is now quite different than it was way back then. That's true of most places in our country and world. A few recently reported examples should suffice:

One hundred years ago . . .

- The average life expectancy for men was forty-seven years.
- Fuel for the 1911 Ford Model T was sold in drugstores only.
- Only 14 percent of the homes in our country had a bathtub. Eight percent had a telephone.
- There were only eight thousand cars and 144 miles of paved roads in the US. The maximum speed limit in most cities was ten mph.
- The average US worker in 1910 earned twenty-two cents per hour and made between $200 and $400 per year.
- More than 95 percent of all births took place at home.
- Ninety percent of all doctors had NO COLLEGE EDUCATION! Instead, they attended so-called medical schools, condemned by many as "substandard."
- Sugar cost four cents a pound. Eggs were fourteen cents a dozen. Coffee was fifteen cents a pound.
- Most women washed their hair once a month and used Borax or egg yolks for shampoo.
- The five leading causes of death were (1) pneumonia and influenza, (2) tuberculosis, (3) diarrhea, (4) heart disease, and (5) stroke.
- There was neither a Mother's Day nor a Father's Day.
- Two out of every ten adults couldn't read or write, and only 6 percent of all Americans had graduated from high school.

While thanking God for the heritage of our past, I also thank Him for the progress of the present! In spite of many difficulties and challenges in our world today, we are truly blessed!

Hakuna Matata! No Worries!

VOLUME III, NUMBER 6—OCTOBER 13, 2011

In 1994, the Walt Disney animated movie *The Lion King* transformed an African phrase into an American household term. *Hakuna matata* is a Swahili expression that means "There are no worries" or, more briefly, "No worries!" In the movie, two jungle animals, Timon and Pumbaa, use this phrase to teach the main character, a lion cub named Simba, to forget his troubled past and live in the present. While Simba eventually learns that lesson, doing so in real life is easier said than done. That's especially true in times of stress, setback, injury, illness, guilt, or grief. How we deal with worry is generally a reflection of our sinful humanity and often a demonstration of the frail and fickle nature of our faith in God.

In a very real way, worry is an affront to God. As Christians, we frequently turn to Him when we experience things that cause humans to worry. Yet, we often delay doing so until all other efforts to remove or alleviate the source of our worries have failed. St. Paul says, "Rejoice always, pray without ceasing, give thanks in all circumstances; for this is the will of God in Christ Jesus for you" (1 Thessalonians 5:16–18). Jesus said, "Do not be anxious about your life [food, clothing, length of life]. . . . Your Father knows that you need [these things]. . . . Instead, seek His kingdom, and these things will be added to you" (Luke 12:22, 30–31).

Sometimes it's difficult to believe that God is paying attention to the things that happen in our lives. Yet actively or passively, in His mercy and grace He allows the circumstances of our lives to occur. And we can live each hour and day trusting in His grace and mercy. That's the only way we can say, "*Hakuna matata!* No worries!"

Reformation

VOLUME III, NUMBER 8—OCTOBER 27, 2011

The Protestant Reformation in the fifteenth and six-teenth centuries aimed to restore the Church, which had become deformed over the course of centuries by false doctrine and wrong practice. This Reformation would bring about the rediscovery of the Gospel of Jesus Christ, endorsing with ringing clarity the great biblical principles of *sola gratia, sola fide, sola scriptura.*

The story of the Reformation is in many ways the story of Martin Luther, whose life basically revolved around his struggle to find peace. Try as he might, Luther could find no peace with God through his own effort and endeavor. Luther's discovery of God's grace was like the proverbial light bulb being illuminated in his mind and heart. This occurred when he read and understood Ephesians 2:8–9, "For by grace you have been saved through faith. And this is not your own doing; it is the gift of God, not a result of works, so that no one may boast." And Romans 1:16, 17, "I am not ashamed of the gospel, for it is the power of God for salvation to everyone who believes. . . . As it is written, 'The righteous shall live by faith.'"

What Luther had uncovered—a biblical truth concealed for centuries—was that faith is not an achievement. It is not something one earns by doing good works or buying indulgences, but it is a *gift* that comes only through the power of the Word of God. This assertion—that salvation comes only by grace through faith in Jesus Christ and not by our own doing—was the upshot of the Protestant Reformation.

Rejoice in the truths of the Reformation we celebrate this week!

Giving Thanks for Grandpa's Hands

VOLUME III, NUMBER 12—NOVEMBER 24, 2011

Today, I want to share a story by an unknown author:

Grandpa, some ninety plus years of age, sat feebly on the patio bench. He didn't move, just sat with his head down staring at his hands. When I sat down beside him, he didn't acknowledge my presence. The longer I sat, the longer I wondered if he was okay. Finally, not really wanting to disturb him but at the same time wanting to check on him, I asked if he was okay. He raised his head and looked at me, smiled, and said in a clear, strong voice, "Yes, I'm fine. Thank you for asking."

"I didn't mean to disturb you, Grandpa, but you were just sitting here staring at your hands and I wanted to make sure you were okay," I explained to him. "Have you ever looked at your hands?" he asked. "I mean, really looked at your hands?" I slowly opened my hands and stared down at them. I turned them over, palms up and then palms down. No, I guess I had never really looked at my hands as I tried to figure out the point he was making.

Grandpa smiled and said, "Stop and think for a moment about the hands you have and how well they have served you throughout your life. When I look at my hands, here are my thoughts:

- These hands, though wrinkled, shriveled, and weak, have been the tools I have used all my life to reach out and embrace life.

- They broke my fall when as a toddler I crashed upon the floor.

- They put food in my mouth and clothes on my back.

- As a child, my mother taught me to fold them in prayer.

- They tied my shoes and pulled on my boots.

- They held my rifle and wiped my tears when I went off to war.

- They have been dirty, scraped and raw, swollen and bent.

- They were uneasy and clumsy when I tried to hold my newborn son.

- Decorated with my wedding band, they showed the world that I was married and loved someone special.

- They wrote the letters home and trembled and shook when I buried your great-grandparents and your grandmother and walked your mother down the aisle.

- Yet they were strong and sure when I dug my buddy out of a foxhole and lifted a plow off my best friend's foot.

- They have held children, consoled neighbors, and shook in fists of anger when I didn't understand.

- They have covered my face, combed my hair, and washed and cleansed the rest of my body.

- They have been sticky and wet, bent and broken, dried and raw.

- And to this day, when not much of anything else of me works real well, these hands hold me up, lay me down, and continue to fold in prayer.

- These hands are the mark of where I've been and the ruggedness of my life.

- But more important, it will be these hands that God will reach out and take when He leads me home.

- With my hands, He will lift me to His side and there I will use these hands to touch the face of Christ."

On this national day of Thanksgiving, give thanks to God for everything He has provided with His almighty hand, including your hands, the hands of those you love, the hands of those who love you, and those who have no hands.

May the peace of our Lord Jesus Christ be with you always!

Advent Reflections

VOLUME III, NUMBER 14—DECEMBER 8, 2011

Can you believe it's already December? One year ago today, Terry and I were supervising the process of unloading furniture and other possessions at our newly purchased home in Georgetown, Texas. Although Advent 2010 had already begun, our attention was focused on other matters. We were busy with the sale of our home in St. Louis and working with the packers and loaders after sorting through things we were keeping and things we were leaving. We were also dealing with the mixture of emotions connected with moving away from wonderful friends in St. Louis and returning to family and dear friends back in Texas.

Advent 2011 began this past Sunday in a way that for our family brought renewed meaning to the coming of Christ—the primary focus of the season. In our family's case, Advent 2011 came on the last day of the earthly life of Frankie Dink Keith, grandfather of our son-in-law, Todd. Dink was eighty-two years old, had been married sixty-four years to his dear Martha, and was dearly loved by many family members and friends, including his great-grandchildren. Two of them also happen to be our grandchildren, Kolby and Kayla. As often happens, this coming of Christ was unannounced, unexpected, unanticipated, adding to the natural emotions of grief and sorrow.

As Paul wrote, "The day of the Lord will come like a thief in the night" (1 Thessalonians 5:2). And Jesus said, "Therefore you also must be ready, for the Son of Man is coming at an hour you do not expect" (Matthew 24:44). Our family's experience this Advent season with the coming of Christ for a man dearly loved brings renewed meaning and understanding to these words, as well as our sorrow at his departure. That sorrow is mitigated by the hope and assurance of eternal life and the resurrection of the body for Dink, a man who knew and loved Christ very dearly. I know full well that our sorrow, hope, and assurance are shared by many.

May the peace of our Lord Jesus Christ be with you always!

Pam's Story

VOLUME III, NUMBER 15—DECEMBER 15, 2011

Pam knows about the pain of considering abortion. More than twenty-one years ago, she and her husband, Bob, were serving as missionaries to the Philippines and praying for a fifth child. Pam contracted amoebic dysentery, an infection of the intestine caused by a parasite found in contaminated food or drink. She went into a coma and was treated with strong antibiotics before they discovered she was pregnant.

Doctors urged her to abort the baby for her own safety and told her that the medicines had caused irreversible damage to her baby. She refused the abortion and cited her Christian faith as the reason for her hope that her son would be born without the devastating disabilities physicians predicted. Pam said the doctors didn't think of it as a life; they thought of it as a mass of fetal tissue.

While pregnant, Pam nearly lost their baby four times but refused to consider abortion. She recalled making a pledge to God with her husband: If you will give us a son, we'll name him Timothy and we'll make him a preacher.

Pam ultimately spent the last two months of her pregnancy in bed and eventually gave birth to a healthy baby boy on August 14, 1987. Pam's youngest son is indeed a preacher. He preaches in prisons, makes hospital visits, and serves with his father's ministry in the Philippines. He also plays football. Pam's son is Tim Tebow.

The University of Florida's star quarterback became the first sophomore in history to win college football's highest award, the Heisman Trophy. His current role as quarterback of the Denver Broncos has provided an incredible platform for Christian witness. As a result, he is being called the Mile-High Messiah.

Tim's notoriety and the family's inspiring story have given Pam numerous opportunities to speak on behalf of women's centers across the country. Pam Tebow believes that every little baby you save matters. May her tribe increase!

Feast and Famine

Volume III, Number 17—December 29, 2011

While Christmas Day of 2011 is now history, the twelve days of Christmas are still coming and going. It didn't take long for TV and newspaper advertisements to pick up where they left off just prior to Christmas, continuing to fuel the flame of commerce, both the traditional in-store variety and also the rapidly expanding trend of e-commerce. Various reports indicate a growing percentage of shoppers each year make their selections and purchases from the comfort of home using a computer, iPad, or any other electronic methodology that works. One well-known national electronics chain had to offer apologies to customers whose purchases would not be delivered in time for Christmas due to the greater than expected volume of pre-Christmas online purchases.

In addition to shopping, on the minds of many folks this first week after Christmas is the matter of holiday weight gain and how to deal with it. That's obvious from the many ads for exercise equipment and weight loss programs we've seen and heard this week. One retired pro football quarterback guest on a late-night TV talk show spent several minutes raving about his loss of thirty-two pounds and his new job promoting the weight reduction product that made his new, more svelte physique possible.

This is only a very small part of the barrage of enticement we're seeing and hearing to purchase anything and everything necessary to help take off the unwanted pounds resulting from all the extra calories consumed at home, office, and neighborhood parties and dinners during the Christmas season. It brings new meaning to the phrase "feast and famine." It's also a very real reminder of the incredible blessings most people in America have received from the hand of our gracious God and, conversely, the ongoing starvation faced by others across the globe. That's a more stark understanding of that same phrase: "feast and famine." We've got our work cut out for us in sharing our feast, both culinary and spiritual, with those who regularly experience famine of both kinds.

Fiscal Contrast, Financial Choice

VOLUME III, NUMBER 18—JANUARY 5, 2012

After coming home from worship New Year's Day, Terry and I relaxed a bit with the Sunday paper and waited for a series of NFL football games by watching a TV program titled *Million Dollar Rooms*. It portrays rooms of all kinds—living rooms, bedrooms, kitchens, game rooms—from obviously superexpensive homes around the world. Some rooms were exquisitely beautiful! Others were just plain vain displays of pulchritudinous possessions. The commercial interruptions were quite different, portraying children in third-world countries alongside appeals for financial contributions of fifty cents per day for UNICEF's support of these children. The contrast was stark between those who somehow have sufficient resources to spend millions of dollars for only one room and those who live every day in extreme poverty and deprivation.

A few days earlier, Terry and I had mailed our special end-of-year contributions to several extracongregational causes. In church that morning, and at a fiftieth anniversary reception that afternoon, my New Year's Day experiences caused me to reflect on the obviously yet undoubtedly unequally blessed people we had seen on TV. In reflecting on our own lives, I felt a sense of quiet thanksgiving to God that His blessings had enabled our collective gifts to be more than I had ever imagined would be possible. I also felt a tinge of guilt that we could have been even more generous, pondering what a huge difference it would make if all the people we had seen that day, including the *Million Dollar Room* owners and the faces we saw in the mirror, would experience the same feelings of fiscal contrast when making financial choices. And I pray that all will respond to the Spirit of God's encouragement to make more than token contributions to worthy charitable causes.

Rendering to Caesar and to God

VOLUME III, NUMBER 33—APRIL 19, 2012

Not long ago, Terry and I visited a congregation of our church body for Sunday morning worship. While walking to our car, I noticed a variety of automobiles in the parking lot. Of course, there were numerous Fords, Chevrolets, Chryslers, Mazdas, Nissans, and Toyotas, in the forms of pickups, vans, and SUVs. There were also quite a few autos bearing the brand of Lexus, Cadillac, BMW, and Mercedes-Benz. I didn't see any Jaguar, Bentley, or Rolls Royce vehicles that particular morning, but I wasn't exactly or intentionally scouring the parking lot.

My observation was part of the conversation in our Volvo on the way home that morning with my dear mother, Elda, and sister Carol. My thoughts included a reminder that many people in the LCMS are obviously richly blessed, some measurably more than others. All four of us commented on counting our blessings with genuine thanksgiving to God. We agreed that it may or may not automatically be a sign of faithfulness to drive a clunker, but neither is it necessarily a sin to drive a very nice or expensive automobile, even what might be considered a luxury vehicle.

Yet I audibly pondered the perpetual reality of financial need experienced by a myriad of not-for-profit entities, including congregations, seminaries, universities, mission agencies, and other charitable endeavors. I also pondered how strange it seems that quite often worthy causes are never known by those in a position to do something helpful about them. It's also rather regrettable that not all who have been blessed with more than necessary or even abundant resources experience the joy of generous, proportionate, intentional, and joyful—not to mention sacrificial—giving.

These thoughts are particularly poignant at this taxing time of year. As most of us know, April 17 was the deadline for filing income tax returns, including not only payment of any balance due but also remittance of estimated tax payments for 2012. That can be a double whammy! A dear friend of mine commented in a recent phone conversation that it's not nearly as much fun to write checks to the United States Treasury or Internal Revenue Service as it is to write checks to his favorite charitable causes. He was quick to add, nevertheless, that paying taxes is still an important reminder of the blessings we have received from our gracious God. I readily agreed.

While nobody I know likes to support governmental leaders or political decisions with which he or she disagrees, or likes to hear news reports about federal, state, or local agencies spending tax dollars wastefully or inappropriately, it's good to recall how blessed we are to live in a country that provides many protections and affords many freedoms. That's what makes the words of Jesus even more pertinent: "Render" (which means "give what is due") "to Caesar the things that are Caesar's, and to God the things that are God's" (Luke 20:25).

Commencement Reflections

VOLUME III, NUMBER 39—MAY 31, 2012

This is the time of year for commencements, which seems like an appropriate reason to take a break from recent Perspectives articles on ecclesiastical matters. It also provides opportunity to congratulate our grandson, Kolby Ryan Keith, who will participate in his Liberty Hill (Texas) High School commencement this weekend—June 1. Actually, his invitation uses the term *graduation*, defined as "the completion of a course of academic study." Indeed, Kolby has done that very well!

The university with which I am currently most familiar—Concordia University Texas in Austin—uses the term *commencement*, defined as "beginning, start, origination, inauguration, instigation, initiation." That makes for an interesting dichotomy between those two terms. One signifies an ending, the other a beginning. In that regard, I've often thought we in the church could do a better job of painting junior confirmation with the brush of commencement—the beginning of a new chapter in a young person's walk of faith—rather than one of graduation, which somehow implies that the confirmand's learning is complete. Not!

Concordia Lutheran High School in Tomball, Texas, held its commencement this past weekend at Salem Lutheran Church in Tomball. They also used the term *commencement*. I was the guest speaker, and in my speech, I made three points to try to depict life as a journey with a series of transitions along the way:

1. Life is not easy.

2. Forgiveness is a precious gift of God.

3. You are a child of God, who is always with you.

It's been said that the best speeches have a strong beginning and a great ending and that the two should be as close together as possible. Mine may have gone a bit longer than the allotted ten minutes, but I had to tell a few stories to support those three points. Hopefully those stories will help the fine young people who walked across the stage and also their parents, grandparents, and other family members and friends remember those simple yet significant truths.

I didn't make the cut as guest speaker at Kolby's graduation/commencement. So I'll just take this opportunity to express my hopes and prayers that he, too, will be continually cognizant of those three realities in his life. Terry and I are very proud of him! We're equally proud of his sister, Kayla, who will do the graduation/ commencement thing next year. Hard to believe both of them are almost grown! Oops! It's more appropriate to say it's hard to believe both of them are approaching a commencement—a beginning of another part of their journey in life.

Faith without Works

Volume III, Number 42—June 21, 2012

One of my greatest concerns is how to respond to the plight of people facing chronic illness, unexpected unemployment, a terminally ill loved one, an estranged spouse, or a rebellious child. It's easy to tell them that they will be in my prayers. It's usually better to stop and pray, right on the spot.

My dear Terry is better at that than I am. Neither of us has ever had a refusal from someone with whom we've offered to pray at a time of grief, guilt, illness, anxiety, uncertainty, depression, or despondency. Indeed, most people for whom prayer is offered remember and appreciate such prayers much longer than the one who offers the prayer.

While I know it is important and effective, at times I feel prayer, even with sincere expression of concern and encouragement, is not enough. I'm haunted by James 2:15–17: "If a brother or sister is poorly clothed and lacking in daily food, and one of you says to them, 'Go in peace, be warmed and filled,' without giving them the things needed for the body, what good is that? So also faith by itself, if it does not have works, is dead." That's probably why I almost never pass a man or woman asking for money at an intersection without giving them something.

So the questions I ask myself are these: Am I doing all I can to aid the sick; comfort the grieving parent, child, widow, or widower; accompany the lonely; feed the hungry; encourage the disconsolate; clothe the nearly naked; support the unwed expectant mother who chooses life over abortion; and patiently counsel those whose lifestyle is different from mine?

And since the answer is *no*, what will motivate me to do more than provide generous financial support to Lutheran social service agencies who pay more daily attention to such matters than I will ever hope to do? And what will cause me to do more than simply give a few dollars to a homeless highway hopeful?

The thought of a dead faith troubles me! The example of the One who gave His very life that my life might be enriched by an abundance of bountiful blessing inspires me! The knowledge that we love because God first loved us motivates me! I hope the same is true for you!

The Wooden Bowl

Volume III, Number 46—July 19, 2012

An unknown author tells a story about a frail old man, who went to live with his son, daughter-in-law, and four-year-old grandson. The old man's hands trembled, his eyesight was blurred, and his step faltered.

The family ate together at the table. But the elderly grandfather's shaky hands and failing sight made eating difficult. Peas rolled off his spoon onto the floor. When he grasped the glass, milk spilled on the tablecloth.

The son and daughter-in-law became irritated with the mess. "We must do something about Father," said the son. "I've had enough of his spilled milk, noisy eating, and food on the floor."

So the husband and wife set a small table in the corner. There, Grandfather ate alone while the rest of the family enjoyed dinner. Since Grandfather had broken a dish or two, his food was served in a wooden bowl.

When the family glanced in Grandfather's direction, sometimes he had a tear in his eye as he sat alone. Still, the only words the couple had for him were sharp admonitions when he dropped a fork or spilled food. The four-year-old watched it all in silence.

One evening before supper, the father noticed his son playing with wood scraps on the floor. He asked the child sweetly, "What are you making?"

Just as sweetly, the boy responded, "Oh, I am making a little bowl for you and Mama to eat your food in when I grow up." The four-year-old smiled and went back to work.

The words so struck the parents that they were speechless. Then tears started to stream down their cheeks. Though no word was spoken, both knew what must be done.

That evening the husband took Grandfather's hand and gently led him back to the family table.

In the Fourth Commandment, God says: "Honor your father and your mother, that your days may be long in the land the LORD your God is giving you" (Exodus 20:12). The same honor should surely also be given to Grandfather and Grandmother!

Surrounded!

VOLUME III, NUMBER 51—AUGUST 23, 2012

This past weekend, I was privileged to preach for the 130th anniversary of Zion Lutheran Church in Walburg, Texas. Whenever I have the opportunity to do so at a congregation that is more than one hundred years old, I usually ask all the charter members to rise. I feel fairly confident that no one will be standing except the preacher (there are almost never any chairs in the pulpit) and perhaps one guy up in the balcony counting the worshipers below. While that question always brings a knowing chuckle, it also very quickly gets the crowd's attention!

As one might expect, I then seize the opportunity to remind the assembly that no one alive at the time that congregation began is still alive today. And I quickly add the obvious: barring some major miracle that magically and significantly extends the current average life span, no one alive today will still be above the ground when this congregation celebrates another centennial anniversary!

And then I usually say something like: "Life is a journey, beginning in our mother's womb and ending in a box that will be buried until the resurrection of all flesh. So as we celebrate this special anniversary, we do so with deep humility, thankful for those who came before us and mindful of those who will come after us."

As the writer of the Letter to the Hebrews says, "We are surrounded by so great a cloud of witnesses" (12:1). You may ask, "So what?" And I will tell you—next week!

May the peace of our Lord Jesus Christ be with you always!

Surrounded! So What?

VOLUME III, NUMBER 52—AUGUST 30, 2012

Last week I quoted from my sermon at a 130th congregational anniversary from the week before: "Life is a journey, beginning in our mother's womb and ending in a box that will be buried until the resurrection of all flesh. So as we celebrate this special anniversary, we do so with deep humility, thankful for those who came before us and mindful of those who will come after us." And then I added: "As the writer of the Letter to the Hebrews says, 'We are surrounded by so great a cloud of witnesses' (12:1). You may ask, 'So what?' And I will tell you—next week!"

So this week I'm keeping that promise. In Hebrews 11, the author begins with this preface: "Now faith is the assurance of things hoped for, the conviction of things not seen. For by it the people of old received their commendation" (11:1–2). The author then lists an impressive slate of Old Testament characters (ancients) and briefly describes challenges each of them had faced, by faith.

That chapter concludes: "All these, though commended through their faith, did not receive what was promised, since God had provided something better for us, that apart from us they should not be made perfect" (11:39–40). The *Concordia Self-Study Bible* says about those last sentences, "All persons of faith who had gone before focused their faith on God and his promises. The fulfillment of God's promises to them has now come in Jesus Christ, and their redemption too is now complete in him" (note on 11:40).[1]

And then begins chapter 12:

> Therefore, since we are surrounded by so great a cloud of
> witnesses, let us also lay aside every weight, and sin which
> clings so closely, and let us run with endurance the race that
> is set before us, looking to Jesus, the founder and perfecter
> of our faith, who for the joy that was set before Him endured
> the cross, despising the shame, and is seated at the right

---

1 *Concordia Self-Study Bible* (St. Louis: Concordia Publishing House, 1986).

hand of the throne of God. Consider Him who endured from sinners such hostility against Himself, so that you may not grow weary or fainthearted. (12:1–3)

Is this cloud of witnesses a fixed, finite group, or does it continue to grow? A friend of mind does an interactive Bible study on this topic. In a follow-up study, Les asks, "So for whom are you a part of the cloud? Others have been part of your cloud—the cloud is not just made up of biblical characters. It includes people who have been a part of your life. And who are the people who would say you are part of their cloud of witnesses?"

That's the blessing of our cloud of witnesses—we are encouraged by their witness and by their example so we will not grow weary and lose heart. In turn, as part of the cloud, we encourage others by our witness and example. It's easy to get discouraged. It's tempting sometimes to give up. But we have this great cloud of witnesses! We are part of that cloud! And we have this Jesus on whom our faith is based, the one who endured the cross!

May the peace of our Lord Jesus Christ be with you always!

Bethlehem

VOLUME IV, NUMBER 5—OCTOBER 4, 2012

Terry and I just returned last week from cohosting a challenging but wonderful Lands of the Bible tour and cruise with our good friend and LCMS Praesidium colleague, Dr. Paul Maier.

It was a challenging trip because right before we left, the US ambassador to Libya was killed. Shortly thereafter, riots ensued in Cairo. The cruise line, Royal Caribbean, wisely decided to skip the Egypt portion of the itinerary, not willing to risk putting anyone in harm's way. Instead of Cairo and Alexandria, we visited beautiful Sicily and Malta.

It was a wonderful trip because of all the historic sites we visited. One very important destination was Bethlehem. Terry and I have been there on two previous occasions, the most recent of which was just a few years ago. A few impressions are indelibly etched in my mind and heart:

1. The Church of the Nativity, possibly the oldest continually operating Christian church in existence, is built over the site thought by many to be the birthplace of Jesus. It now is full of not very professionally installed eternal lights and other accoutrements that are almost gauche in appearance. But there is a palpable sense of awe discernible from the attention being paid by tourists to guides describing via individual communication devices the scene and its importance. There's no mistaking the reason these people have come here from around the world. This is the place where the most important person in the history of the world was born—Jesus, our Savior!

2. Just down the street from the Church of the Nativity is Christmas Lutheran Church, which was the focus of our Holy Land trip a few years ago. Pastor Mitri Raheb has led the development of a vitally significant ministry, including very

fine facilities for health care, education, and economic development. This ministry is supported in America by a group called Bright Stars of Bethlehem, including a goodly number of LCMS men and women. Though we were unable to revisit these facilities on this trip, we can't go to Bethlehem without thanking God for its important ministry of Lutherans in the Holy Land.

3. Just across the street from the Church of the Nativity is a Muslim mosque; I became aware of this a few years ago. We were staying at the Christmas Lutheran Church retreat center and were rudely awakened at 5:00 a.m. by loud chanting that I soon discovered was the Muslim call to prayer. That was merely one reminder that the population in the city of our Lord's birth is only 10 to 15 percent Christian, which is very disturbing, to say the least!

4. Due to political tensions between Israel and Palestine, a giant, ugly, oppressive concrete wall has been built around the entire West Bank. It appears to be at least twenty feet tall and is punctuated only by a few checkpoints through which all who enter or leave Bethlehem must pass. The wall is several years old and has begun to be covered with graffiti, some quite artistic, others just plain ugly. I wonder how long it will take for tensions to be resolved to the point that a US president or some other influential individual will echo Ronald Reagan's plea to Mikhail Gorbachev, General Secretary of the Communist Party of the Soviet Union, on June 12, 1987: "Tear down this wall."

5. Notwithstanding the unhappy realities noted above, I recall with joy and hope the prophetic words of Micah 5, fulfilled in this city that today faces many challenges:

But you, O Bethlehem Ephrathah, . . . from you shall come forth for Me one who is to be ruler in Israel. . . . And He shall stand and shepherd His flock in the strength of the LORD, in the majesty of the name of the LORD His God. And they shall dwell secure, for now He shall be great to the ends of the earth. (5:2, 4)

Jesus Loves Me! He Also Loves You!

VOLUME IV, NUMBER 10—NOVEMBER 8, 2012

A recent email tells of a church in Atlanta that honored one of its senior pastors who had been retired many years. He was ninety-two at the time. After a warm welcome, the man placed both hands on the pulpit to steady himself and then quietly and slowly began to speak:

> When I was asked to come here today and talk to you, your pastor asked me to tell you what was the greatest lesson ever learned in my more than fifty years of preaching. I thought about it for a few days and boiled it down to just one thing that made the most difference in my life and sustained me through all my trials. The one thing that I could always rely on to bring comfort when tears, pain, heartbreak, fear, and sorrow paralyzed me was this verse of a familiar song:

Jesus loves me! This I know,
For the Bible tells me so.
Little ones to Him belong;
They are weak, But He is strong.
Yes, Jesus loves me!
Yes, Jesus loves me!
Yes, Jesus loves me!
The Bible tells me so. (*LSB* 588:1)

Here is a new version, just for folks who have white hair or no hair at all. For those of us over middle age and all you others as well, check out this newest version of "Jesus Loves Me" (author unknown):

Jesus loves me, this I know, though my hair is white as snow,
Though my sight is growing dim, still He bids me trust in Him.
Though my steps are oh, so slow, with my hand in His I'll go

On through life, let come what may, He'll be there to lead the way.
When the nights are dark and long, in my heart He puts a song
Telling me in words so clear: "Have no fear, for I am near."

When my work on earth is done and life's victories have been won
He will take me home above. Then I'll understand His love.
I love Jesus, does He know? Have I ever told Him so?
Jesus loves to hear me say that I love Him every day.
YES, JESUS LOVES ME! YES, JESUS LOVES ME!
YES, JESUS LOVES ME! THE BIBLE TELLS ME SO!

Yes, Jesus loves me! He also loves you! May the peace of our Lord Jesus Christ be with you always!

A Difficult Time

VOLUME IV, NUMBER 14—DECEMBER 6, 2012

It was a difficult time. Election to a national leadership position in the summer of 2001 meant that Terry and I would sell our home in Texas and say goodbye to family, other loved ones, and many friends. We moved to St. Louis, home of the International Center of The Lutheran Church—Missouri Synod, in late August of that year.

Installation to the Office of the President of the LCMS took place Saturday, September 8. Three days later, on September 11, terrorists struck the World Trade Center towers in New York City and three other places in the US. Our country and world would never be the same.

As all these changes and challenges were occurring, a regular physical exam and subsequent procedures determined that prostate cancer had developed in my otherwise very healthy body. After prayer and consultation, I decided to undergo a radical prostatectomy (no robotic da Vinci procedures were available then) on November 26, 2001, eleven years ago last week.

Barnes-Jewish Hospital in St. Louis had a good reputation. So did my surgeon, Dr. William Catalona. He had been largely responsible for developing the PSA test, widely used to determine the possible presence of prostate cancer. Those important details were positive and encouraging.

But Terry and I felt frightened and alone. I had never before (nor since) undergone major surgery. We were in a new place, away from family and most close friends who were left behind in Texas, understandably worried and feeling helpless.

We were very thankful for the wonderful support and prayers of family and friends. By the grace of God, the surgery was successful. The cancer had not spread beyond the prostate gland. No further treatment was necessary. No physical impairment resulted.

Today I'm very concerned about and supportive of men whose diagnoses mirror mine, and I often call and pray with them. Terry does the same with wives who face what she faced. Encouragement and support of patient and spouse are important.

It was a difficult time in our lives. You have difficult times in your life. Throughout these times, to whom do we turn for hope? We can do nothing other than place our trust and confidence in the God who knows, who loves, who cares!

The House That Built Me

VOLUME IV, NUMBER 15—DECEMBER 13, 2012

In "The House That Built Me," singer Miranda Lambert goes back to the home of her childhood. She persuades the current owner to allow this brief walk down memory lane, assuring the owner that she won't take anything from the house except her memories. She recalls in the song several pivotal places, moments, memories, and events from the past.

- Her handprints in the concrete of the front steps
- The little upstairs back bedroom where she did homework and learned to play guitar
- The live oak tree under which her favorite dog is buried in the yard
- The house plans her mama cut out for years from *Better Homes and Gardens* magazine

All of us have memories of the home of our childhood. In my case, there were two of them. One still stands, remodeled beyond recognition. Over the years, the neighborhood has changed from rural to ghetto to mixed commercial. A couple weeks ago Terry and I drove past it, bringing to mind some memories of this home:

- It apparently had been a bookie joint for twenty-five years before Mom and Dad bought it.
- Our family spent the next twenty-five years remodeling and adding on to it.
- The three acres on which it stood were home to numerous FFA projects, animals, and crops.
- It had two stories, an unpaved horseshoe driveway, and concrete front porch steps against which I spent hours throwing a golf ball, catching the rebound with my baseball glove.
- When it was sold, the next owners turned it into a nightclub called The Total Experience!

- It i's now a commercial building that bears little resemblance to the home of my childhood.

In addition to much hard work and many happy experiences with my parents and three sisters, one thing I clearly recall in the house is the plaque that had a prominent position on one of the walls: "Only one life, 'twill soon be past. Only what's done for Christ will last!"

And that's what I remember most about the house that built me!

Peace on Earth and Evil in Connecticut

Volume IV, Number 16—December 20, 2012

This article was intended to have a distinctly Christmas focus. However, the events of the past week demand attention. In the midst of preparations for celebrating the joyful occasion of the birth of Jesus and the announcement by the angels to the shepherds of "good news of great joy" (Luke 2:10), many lives have been disrupted by evil in Connecticut. Yet, by the grace of God, our hearts are comforted with hope from one special portion of the angelic message: "On earth peace" (Luke 2:14)!

By now, most people alive today know about the evil that visited Newtown, Connecticut, this past Friday. A twenty-year-old man shot and killed his mother. Then he went to Sandy Hook Elementary School and violently snuffed out the lives of twenty defenseless six- and seven-year-old children, along with six adults—teachers and other school personnel, including the school principal. The Newtown community and our entire nation mourn the tragic and senseless loss of these precious lives.

On the day of that trauma, Connecticut Governor Dan Malloy said: "Evil visited this community today." In Ephesians 6:12, the apostle Paul confirms his assessment: "We do not wrestle against flesh and blood, but against . . . the cosmic powers over this present darkness, against the spiritual forces of evil in the heavenly places." This dastardly deed was done not just by a deranged young man, but by a person whom spiritual forces of satanic evil used to devour innocent children and adults.

Much has been and will continue to be written about what needs to be done to stop these senseless massacres that occur all too often, particularly in our country. Gun control, especially concerning weapons such as the AR-15 used last week, will certainly become a more prominent topic of conversation. So will the treatment of the types of mental illness that spawn both spontaneous and strategic violence. Other subjects also beg for attention.

We need to address seriously the deterioration of the family and the decline of basic Christian values in our country and world. Next on the list would be the flood of violent movies, internet sites, TV programs, and video games that numb the mind and desensitize the conscience of people filled with rage who have the propensity to replicate what happened in Newtown, Connecticut.

In the meantime, we try to make sense of a senseless act of terror—an impossible task in itself and difficult even in the light of God's promises. Yet, it's critical that we remember and speak these promises, especially to those who grieve. They are far more than simply words—they are the promises of God:

- Romans 8:28: "We know that for those who love God all things work together for good, for those who are called according to His purpose."

- Romans 8:38–39: "For I am sure that neither death nor life, nor angels nor rulers, nor things present nor things to come, nor powers, nor height nor depth, nor anything else in all creation, will be able to separate us from the love of God in Christ Jesus our Lord."

- 1 Corinthians 15:26: "The last enemy to be destroyed is death."

- 1 Corinthians 15:54–57: "'Death is swallowed up in victory.' 'O death, where is your victory? O death, where is your sting?' The sting of death is sin, and the power of sin is the law. But thanks be to God, who gives us the victory through our Lord Jesus Christ."

- Revelation 2:10: "Be faithful unto death, and I will give you the crown of life."

- Revelation 21:4: "[God] will wipe away every tear from their eyes, and death shall be no more, neither shall there be mourning, nor crying, nor pain anymore, for the former things have passed away."

Equipped with and encouraged by those eternal promises, we seek to honor God's precious gift of life by concerning ourselves, to the greatest extent humanly possible, with matters of precaution against and prevention of future eruptions of evil. To that we add the very important matter of ongoing prayer and support for the families affected by last week's atrocity.

May God's Spirit help each of us turn our hearts back to the words of the angels to the shepherds: "Glory to God in the highest, and on earth peace among those with whom He is pleased" (Luke 2:14).

Terry and I pray for you and your family a special measure of the peace from Christ that passes all understanding—God's Christmas peace on earth, even in the wake of evil in Connecticut.

May the peace of our Lord Jesus Christ be with you always!

Giving and Receiving

VOLUME IV, NUMBER 17—DECEMBER 27, 2012

For as long as I can recall, our family has chosen the night before Christmas for giving and receiving gifts during this festive season. While it has evolved over the years, our current routine is to attend an early Christmas Eve service, return home for Terry's scrumptious lasagna and trimmings, open our presents, and conclude the evening with mint dazzler for dessert.

This week in my prayer before our Christmas Eve meal, I thanked God for his gift of those who have gone before us, including my father and Terry's mother, father, and stepfather. All of us have received much from each of them, including my still very much alive 96½-year-old mother, Elda. We've learned lessons of life and love and that it is more blessed to give than to receive.

In my prayer I also included those in our country and world who do not have the financial resources to purchase anything we might consider worthy of giving. And many of them do not know anyone from whom they might receive any tangible Christmas gift. So for them, giving to others is a luxury preempted by the daily stress of finding food for sustenance and survival.

With this in mind, a tradition of great joy for us in this season is writing above-and-beyond end-of-year checks to our favorite charitable causes. Almost all of them are church related, providing professional, compassionate, missional, educational ministry for people in our country and world. Many of you also find joy in this practice and join me in encouraging others to do the same.

During this holy season, we do well to realize what a privilege it is to be able both to give and to receive. And in the process of thanking God for His greatest gift to mankind—our Savior, Jesus, born in a manger in Bethlehem—we are especially blessed to express in a tangible way our conviction that it is indeed better to give than to receive!

In Loving Memory

VOLUME IV, NUMBER 18—JANUARY 3, 2013

This New Year's week article is written in loving memory of fathers who have already left this life, including mine. While not all have pleasant memories of life with their father, my siblings and I give thanks to God for that wonderful blessing.

New Year's Day of 2013 marked the thirtieth anniversary of the passing of my beloved father, Martin Herbert Otto Kieschnick. He was a faithful husband, father, and grandfather who loved the Lord. When church doors were open, he and his family were almost always there. During the entirety of my childhood, I don't remember ever failing to attend Sunday worship and Sunday School.

Dad's vocation was meat cutter, and his avocation was meat cooker. At church picnics, he grilled chickens for hundreds of people on a huge homemade grill of chicken wire stretched across rebar over a freshly dug open pit in the ground. Handy with his hands, he was a do-it-yourselfer who loved to renovate, improve, and add on to our home. No project was too big. Anything he could envision and afford, he could build.

Dad and Mom (she's still enthusiastic, effervescent, and energetic at 96 ½ years and going strong) were far from wealthy during our childhood. But by the grace of God and with a lot of hard work, they were able to provide for their three daughters and one son. We didn't wear fancy clothing and always drove reliably undependable used cars. But we never missed a meal.

Many times in the three decades since Dad's death I've recalled things he said during his lifetime. Here are a few:

- Don't work harder, work smarter!
- One woman is enough for a real man!
- You can't have great barbecue if you don't start with a good piece of meat!
- You can't out-give the Lord—He has a bigger shovel than you do!

Much more could be said about the man I was privileged to call Dad. He would be the first to admit that he was not without original sin. But he knew and cherished God's grace and forgiveness. Although Father's Day is several months away, every day I give thanks to God for my father.

Recalling fathers who are gone and thankful for those who remain, consider the sage advice in selected verses of Proverbs:

- "The fear of the LORD is the beginning of knowledge" (1:7)

- "A wise son hears his father's instruction" (13:1)

- "A wise son makes a glad father" (15:20)

- "Listen to your father who gave you life" (23:22)

- "He who fathers a wise son will be glad in him" (23:24)

May the peace of our Lord Jesus Christ be with you always!

Public Profanity

VOLUME IV, NUMBER 21—JANUARY 24, 2013

Maybe I'm becoming more narrow-minded and cranky as I grow older. Perhaps my conservative colors are showing even more brightly than before. Or it could just be the lingering effect of the one and only time, many years ago, that my mother washed out my mouth with soap—YUCK!!!

Whatever the cause, the ax I'm grinding in this article is the proliferation of public profanity in our country. Words unfit for either private utterance or public consumption are becoming more and more common. At least that's my experience. And it's not just in conversations between two people or in small groups. It's also commonplace on TV and rampant in the movies.

What's the reason for the frequent and flippant use of vulgar terminology? Perhaps it's simply a bad habit. Or maybe folks who flavor their conversation with unsavory words are just lazy or ignorant or insensitive. In some cases, it's all of the above. In other cases, peer pressure prevails. In all cases, sin is both the cause and the result.

I'm not talking here about the occasional slip of the tongue, especially when, for example, a hammer smashes a finger. Certain things or events evoke disgust that leads to inappropriate emotional expression. I understand that reality and am not above reproach in that regard.

What I'm talking about here is frequent, regular use of foul, dirty, vulgar words that are offensive and distasteful. Personally speaking, my ears are greatly offended by language that curses God, damns people, or denigrates certain God-given sexual activity.

A very small article in an obscure part of an interior page of a back section of the June 13, 2012, issue of the *Austin American Statesman* caught my eye. Its title was: "Town to assess fines for public profanity." Here's what it said about Middleborough, Massachusetts: "Residents in Middleborough have voted to make people pay fines for swearing in public. At a town meeting Monday night, residents voted 183-50 to approve a plan to impose a twenty dollar fine on public profanity. Officials insist the plan isn't intended to censor casual or private conversations, but instead to crack down on loud profanity used in public."

It's interesting that this action was taken by a civic entity. I wonder what the reaction would be to a similar decision or public statement by a religious body. My encouragement is for pastors, parents, and teachers to continue to speak frankly and fearlessly to children, to one another, and to everyone else about the importance of and proper respect for chaste and decent language.

Achieving such is no simple task, as acknowledged even long ago by a biblical writer: "No human being can tame the tongue. It is a restless evil, full of deadly poison. With it we bless our Lord and Father, and with it we curse people who are made in the likeness of God. From the same mouth come blessing and cursing. My brothers, these things ought not to be so" (James 3:8–10).

The Folded Linen

Volume IV, Number 32—March 28, 2013

The days of Holy Week are special opportunities for worship and reflection on our Lord Jesus:

- Maundy Thursday: observing the anniversary of His institution of the Lord's Supper

- Good Friday: focusing on His crucifixion, death, and burial

- Holy Saturday: commemorating the full day Jesus lay in His tomb

- The Festival of the Resurrection: celebrating the rising of Jesus from the dead

As our thoughts and hearts are directed toward these significant events, interesting questions arise from time to time regarding the details. For example, why did Jesus fold the linen burial cloth after His resurrection? A story I recently read offered the following explanation.

The Gospel of John (20:7) tells us that the napkin, which was placed over the face of Jesus, was not just thrown aside like the grave clothes. The Bible takes an entire verse to tell us that the napkin was neatly folded and was placed at the head of that stony coffin.

Early Sunday morning while it was still dark, Mary Magdalene came to the tomb and found that the stone had been rolled away from the entrance. She ran and found Simon Peter and the other disciple (undoubtedly John), the one whom Jesus loved. She said: "They have taken the Lord out of the tomb, and we do not know where they have laid Him" (John 20:2).

Peter and the other disciple ran to the tomb to see. The other disciple outran Peter and got there first. He stooped and looked in and saw the linen cloth lying there, but he didn't go in.

Then Simon Peter arrived and went inside. He also noticed the linen wrappings lying there while the cloth that had covered Jesus' head was folded up and lying in a place by itself.

Was that important? Absolutely! Is it really significant? Yes!

In order to understand the significance of the folded napkin, one needs to understand a little bit about Jewish tradition of that day. The folded napkin had to do with the master and servant, and every Jewish boy knew this tradition.

When the servant set the dinner table for the master, he made sure that it was exactly the way the master wanted it. The table was furnished perfectly. Then the servant would wait just out of sight until the master had finished eating, and the servant would not dare touch that table until the master was finished.

Now if the master were done eating he would rise from the table, wipe his fingers and mouth, clean his beard, and wad up that napkin and toss it onto the table. The servant would then know to clear the table. For in those days, the wadded napkin meant: *I'm finished.*

But if the master got up from the table and folded his napkin and laid it beside his plate, the servant would not dare touch the table because the folded napkin meant: *I'm coming back!*

AND SO HE WILL! We confess our belief about Jesus in the Apostles' Creed: "The third day He rose again from the dead. He ascended into heaven and sits at the right hand of God the Father Almighty. From thence He will come to judge the living and the dead" (Second Article).

Terry and I pray for each of you a very meaningful Holy Week and a most blessed Festival of the Resurrection of our Lord, aka Easter Sunday!

May the peace of our Lord Jesus Christ be with you always!

Scars on the Ground

VOLUME IV, NUMBER 40—MAY 23, 2013

While I cannot speak for anyone but myself, I'm fairly certain I'm not the only one who is terribly saddened, even to the point of (at least for me) nonclinical depression from the news of yet another disaster resulting in trauma, tragedy, and tears. Such is the case with this week's reports of the devastating tornado that hit Moore, Oklahoma, this past Monday, May 20.

At the time this article is being written, twenty-four deaths have been reported, including a number of children. Hundreds were injured and others may still be missing. Those numbers may well have changed by the time you read this article.

Hospitals and schools were destroyed. Entire subdivisions were obliterated. Property damage is unfathomable. Loss of a lifetime of possessions is unimaginable. Human life is irreplaceable.

One report that came to my attention noted observations of a helicopter pilot surveying the area. It described entire neighborhoods swept clean—no homes, no trees, just scars on the ground.

Questions always arise at a time like this. For me and many others, the biggest one is "Why does God allow natural disasters?" This question haunts thinking and feeling people of faith and stirs greater doubt in people for whom faith is a huge challenge, even when peace and normality exist.

In "Natural Disasters: A Biblical Perspective" (http://www.ucg.org/news-and-prophecy/natural-disasters-biblical-perspective/), Tom Robinson lists sixteen points to keep in mind concerning the biblical perspective on tragedies, regardless of their scale or circumstances. While it would be difficult for a Lutheran Christian to agree with all sixteen points, several are worthy of mention:

- God has said in Bible prophecy that natural disasters would grow in frequency and intensity as the end of the age approaches—to shake people out of their complacency and lead them to seek Him (Matthew 24:7; Luke 21:25–26; Revelation 6:12; 11:13; 16:18).

- Those who die in accidents or natural disasters are not necessarily greater sinners than those who survive (Luke 13:1–5).

- Natural disasters or accidents should humble us, helping us to see our dependence on God to sustain and deliver us (Revelation 16:8–11).

- We don't know all the reasons God brings or permits specific calamities or why particular people are made to suffer by them, but we should trust that in God's omniscience and ultimate wisdom He knows how to work out what is best for everyone in the end (Romans 8:28; 1 Timothy 2:4).

Especially this week, my heart is with those who used to live in neighborhoods that were "swept clean—no homes, no trees, just scars on the ground." Those scars on the ground were left by a horrendous storm that devastated property and destroyed possessions. Yet God's people are still precious to Him. Much more than scars on the ground, we are His priceless children!

May the peace of our Lord Jesus be with you always! And may that peace be with our friends in Oklahoma and others for whom peace is seemingly, at least for the moment, an elusive dream.

How About a Few More Rules for Teachers?

VOLUME V, NUMBER 2—AUGUST 29, 2013

Last week I wrote about "Rules for Women Teachers" in 1915, which many of you forwarded to friends and family. Before leaving the topic of rules for teachers from the past, it seemed appropriate to mention one more set. Here we go, with permission again from Zion Lutheran Church in Wayside, Wisconsin.

RULES FOR TEACHERS—1872

1. Teachers each day will fill lamps and clean chimneys.

2. Each teacher will bring a bucket of water and scuttle of coal for the day's session.

3. Make your pens carefully. You may whittle nibs to the individual taste of the pupils.

4. Men teachers may take one evening each week for courting purposes, or two evenings a week if they go to church regularly.

5. After ten hours in school, the teachers may spend the remaining time reading the Bible or other good books.

6. Women teachers who marry or engage in unseemly conduct will be dismissed.

7. Every teacher should lay aside from each pay a goodly sum of earnings for his benefit during his declining years so that he will not become a burden to society.

8. Any teacher who smokes, uses liquor in any form, frequents pool or public halls, or gets shaved in a barber shop will have given reason to suspect his worth, intention, integrity and honesty.

9. The teacher who performs his labor faithfully and without fault for five years will be given an increase of twenty-five cents per week in his pay, providing the Board of Education approves.

Folks, I'm not making up this stuff! This is real! A few of these rules particularly caught my eye and I suspect you noticed them also. Unseemly conduct is not an everyday household term. And I suppose any male teacher who was romantically interested in a young lady would be motivated, properly or improperly, to be in church on a regular basis—"regular" being a term not defined in the rules, but probably meaning every week, without fail. Sounds perfectly reasonable to me!

But the two rules most poignantly on my mind right now are numbers 7 and 9. Both have to do with teachers' compensation, current and future. This is a topic of importance still today.

Since I'm out of the ecclesiastical supervision and church/school personnel business, I don't hear nearly as much about this matter these days as in the past. However, I suspect the issue of compensation for church workers, perhaps particularly educators and other commissioned ministers of the Gospel, is still a matter of concern. Worries about resources during declining years have lessened significantly as a result of Concordia Plan Services, which includes the LCMS retirement plan. Social Security, for those who have participated, also helps significantly.

But I believe the fact remains that educators and other commissioned workers are far too often compensated below the intrinsic value of the ministry to which they commit their time, heart, and soul. As a result, many church workers face retirement without sufficient financial resources for comfortable living, with luxuries simply remaining out of the question.

"The laborer deserves his wages" (1 Timothy 5:18) or words quite similar are mentioned many times in Holy Scripture. If you'd like to take a look, here's a partial list of references: 1 Corinthians 9:9; Deuteronomy 25:4; Matthew 10:10; Luke 10:7; Leviticus 19:13; Deuteronomy 24:15; 1 Corinthians 9:4, 7–14.

With that motivation, my encouragement is for church leaders at every level to inquire into the compensation of all those who serve in congregational ministry, including educational, musical, custodial, and pastoral staff. Compensation levels should be more than just adequate. Pay scales provided by regional judicatories are almost always designed to be minimum recommendations.

If adjustments need to be made, have the courage to urge that the right thing be done as quickly as possible. That may very well include an honest look at your own level of personal financial stewardship and an encouragement for fellow congregational members to do the same.

Remember that we have been blessed to be a blessing and to honor God in all we do, with all we are and with all we have! We are called to do so in a twenty-first-century context, which we all know is radically different from the way things were and the way things were viewed in 1872!

Senseless, Needless Evil

VOLUME V, NUMBER 3—SEPTEMBER 5, 2013

Nidal Malik Hasan is a United States Army Medical Corps officer who fatally shot thirteen people and injured thirty-two others in a mass shooting at Fort Hood, Texas, on November 5, 2009. On August 23, 2013, a jury panel convicted him of thirteen counts of premeditated murder and thirty-two counts of attempted murder. On August 28, a panel of thirteen military officers sentenced him to death.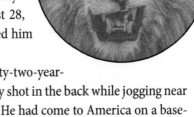

On August 16, Christopher Lane, a twenty-two-year-old native of Melbourne, Australia, was fatally shot in the back while jogging near his girlfriend's home in Duncan, Oklahoma. He had come to America on a baseball scholarship at East Central University in Ada, Oklahoma.

Three boys—ages 15, 16, and 17—are charged with what prosecutors call a "thrill killing." Two are being charged with first-degree murder, as adults. The third is charged with using a vehicle in the discharge of a weapon and accessory to first-degree murder.

On August 21, an eighty-eight-year-old World War II veteran was savagely beaten by two teenagers in a parking lot in Spokane, Washington. Two male suspects assaulted Delbert Belton for no apparent reason. He died the next morning from injuries sustained in the brutal attack.

"Shorty," as he was known by his friends, served in the US Army in the Pacific during WWII and was shot in the leg during the Battle of Okinawa. Two teenagers have been arrested and charged with first-degree robbery and first-degree murder, with additional teenagers arrested and charged with rendering criminal assistance.

No matter how many times I read or hear similar stories, I'm shocked and dismayed by the senseless, needless, evil nature of these brutal crimes. All too often, but not always, the culprits are young men who perpetrate their dastardly deeds with little or no provocation or motive. In one of the cases above, the violators described themselves simply as "bored." In other cases, sheer terrorism, motivated by misguided religious principles or promises, is the cause.

In addition to these cases, we hear and see on TV news reports and video the hundreds, even thousands, of mostly young men who comprise the throngs of riotous demonstrators in places such as Cairo, Egypt, and Damascus, Syria. Those demonstrations are violent and often deadly, evoking puzzlement and dismay at the absence of respect for life in their demeanor and behavior.

In all these cases, loved ones and family members of the victims are the ones who truly pay the price. I wish I could offer hope that these senseless, needless, evil killings would stop. Sadly and for many reasons, I doubt that will be the case.

Satan still walks about "like a roaring lion, seeking someone to devour. Resist him, firm in your faith, knowing that the same kinds of suffering are being experienced by your brotherhood throughout the world" (1 Peter 5:8–9).

Lord, have mercy!

New Year Reflections

VOLUME V, NUMBER 20—JANUARY 1, 2014

Every New Year's Day for the past thirty-one years I've reflected on an event that occurred January 1, 1983. My dear father, Martin Herbert Otto Kieschnick, went to heaven that day at the tender age of sixty-six years, six months, two days. I miss him every day and thank God for his influence in my life.

That influence continues to be exerted upon our entire family through my dear mother, Elda Mary Hellman Kieschnick, now ninety-seven years, eight months, twenty days of age. With the significant exception of Dad's passing and in light of Mom's effervescent spirit and cheerful outlook on life, most of my New Year's thoughts look through a windshield, not a rearview mirror.

The *Complete Speaker's Almanac* points out that the month of January is named after the Roman god Janus: "This particular Roman god had two faces, enabling him to look ahead toward the future and back at the past at the same time. As we get rid of an old year and look forward to a new one, we all try to be a little like Janus. We know through experience what we did wrong and what we did right, and hope to do better this year. Some people make ambitious New Year's resolutions; others just take a deep breath and hope for the best."

How about you? Are you looking back or looking ahead? Are you making ambitious New Year's resolutions or just hoping for the best? Resolutions have a way of losing their urgency shortly after the New Year rolls around. And I've never been one simply to hope for the best without trying to do what I felt necessary for the best to occur, with God's abundant blessing. My reflections and projections, hopes and prayers for the New Year go hand in hand.

With that in mind, I share with you "A New Year's Wish" from an unknown author:

> *May God make your year a happy one!*
> *Not by shielding you from all sorrows and pain, but by strengthening you to bear it, as it comes;*

Not by making your path easy, but by making you sturdy to travel any path;

Not by taking hardships from you, but by taking fear from your heart;

Not by granting you unbroken sunshine, but by keeping your face bright, even in the shadows;

Not by making your life always pleasant, but by showing you when people and their causes need you most, and by making you anxious to be there to help.

And "A New Year's Prayer," also from an unknown author:

Spirit of the risen Christ, be with us today and always.
Be our Light, our Guide, and our Comforter.
Be our Strength, our Courage, and our Sanctifier.
May this New Year be a time of deep spiritual growth: a time of welcoming Your graces and gifts; a time for forgiving freely and unconditionally; a time for growing in virtue and goodness.
Come, Holy Spirit! Be with us today and always! Amen!

Terry and I pray God's abundant love, peace, hope, and joy will come to you in the year ahead!

MLK Day

VOLUME V, NUMBER 23—JANUARY 23, 2014

When I was a kid, there was no such thing as Martin Luther King Jr. Day. It's now a federal holiday on the third Monday of January each year, commemorating Dr. King's birthday, January 15, 1929. President Ronald Reagan signed the holiday into law in 1983, and it was first observed three years later, in 1986. Only two other people have national holidays in the United States honoring them: George Washington and Christopher Columbus.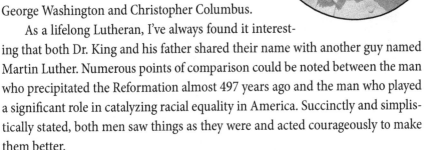

As a lifelong Lutheran, I've always found it interesting that both Dr. King and his father shared their name with another guy named Martin Luther. Numerous points of comparison could be noted between the man who precipitated the Reformation almost 497 years ago and the man who played a significant role in catalyzing racial equality in America. Succinctly and simplistically stated, both men saw things as they were and acted courageously to make them better.

From my younger days, I vividly recall the visual reminders of absolute segregation:

- People with a darker complexion than the rest of us were not allowed to ride anywhere other than the back of the bus.

- They were forbidden to enter public restaurants and stores.

- In stores and other public places, there were three restrooms: Women, Men, Colored.

- "Colored people" could not attend our schools. I don't recall seeing one African-American student or faculty member on campus at Houston's Bellaire High School or at Texas A&M, the latter of which admitted five African-American freshmen to the A&M Corps of Cadets the semester following my graduation in 1964.

- While there were African-American pastors in the LCMS, we had none in my 1970 Concordia Theological Seminary graduating class in

Springfield, Illinois. I perceive and believe that was the result of a set of factors quite different from absolute segregation.

My 1964 college graduation coincided with the Civil Rights Act of 1964 and preceded Dr. King's assassination on April 4, 1968. Since that time, slowly but surely, racial integration in America has progressed to where it is today. While racial prejudice still exists in many forms, I thank God that, for most Americans, racial equality has become a way of life.

Sadly, that cannot be said universally. In many countries of the world, racial prejudice still rears its ugly head. It manifests itself in various ways, including the same kind of violence that took the life of Dr. Martin Luther King Jr. over forty-five years ago. Lord, have mercy!

St. Paul had it right when he wrote: "There is neither Jew nor Greek, there is neither slave nor free, there is no male and female, for you are all one in Christ Jesus" (Galatians 3:28).

The peace of the Lord be with you all!

Super Bowl Reflections

VOLUME V, NUMBER 25—FEBRUARY 6, 2014

Unless you've been in a cave the past few weeks, you are aware that this past Sunday was Super Bowl XLVIII. For folks unfamiliar with Roman numerals, all those capital letters can be more succinctly expressed with the number forty-eight.

This annual championship game of the National Football League began with the first such contest on January 15, 1967. The athletic history buffs among us will recall that the Green Bay Packers won the first two Super Bowls, defeating the Kansas City Chiefs and the Oakland Raiders in 1967 and 1968 respectively. I don't remember that detail. I just read it on the Internet.

It has not been uncommon for interesting things to happen at Super Bowls, whether during the game or the halftime show, which has historically been quite elaborate. A few examples will suffice:

- New York Giants QB Phil Simms shouted, "I'm going to Disney World," after his MVP performance in 1987. Disney CEO Michael Eisner paid Simms $75,000 for the ad.

- A highly publicized "wardrobe malfunction" at halftime during Super Bowl XXXVIII in 2004 occurred when male singer Justin Timberlake exposed an anatomical part of female singer Janet Jackson before a television audience of millions.

- Although the words were on the jumbotron in front of her, Grammy-winning singer Christina Aguilera botched the words to the national anthem in 2011.

- A partial power outage during the third quarter caused a thirty-four minute delay in the game during the 2013 Super Bowl XLVII in New Orleans.

- Especially in recent years, corporations have generated creative advertisements costing four million dollars per thirty seconds. Many viewers pay more attention to the commercials than to the game.

More significantly, over the years, some Super Bowl stars, mostly from the winning team, have given clear and courageous Christian testimonies following the game. Two examples suffice:

Following the St. Louis Rams' Super Bowl XXXIV victory, Kurt Warner, the game MVP, responded to a question from an ABC reporter: "Well, first things first. I've got to thank my Lord and Savior up above—thank You, Jesus!"

Nine years later, upon leading the Arizona Cardinals to the franchise's first ever Super Bowl, Warner's response was similar: "Everybody's going to be tired of hearing this, but I never get tired of saying it. There's one reason that I'm standing up on this stage today. That's because of my Lord up above. I've got to say thanks to Jesus."

And this year's Super Bowl winning quarterback, Russell Wilson, in a post-game interview, said: "It's a true, true blessing. God is so good." Russell also quoted his father: "Believe in the talent God has given you . . . and you can go a long ways."

Both athletes seized the opportunity to give thanks to God in a highly public manner. I thank God whenever that happens!

The World's Wealthiest

VOLUME V, NUMBER 32—MARCH 27, 2014

The *Austin American Statesman* published an article by Matthew Schofield on January 21, 2014, citing a report by the British-based antipoverty charity Oxfam. It stated that the eighty-five richest people in the world own half the world's wealth. The report's observation was, "The world's poorest 3.55 billion people must live on what the richest 85 possess." It also reported, "The wealth of the one percent of the richest people in the world amounts to $110 trillion." That number looks like this: $110,000,000,000,000.

In addition, a March 3, 2014, report by *Forbes* magazine identified the world's richest people, stating that there are 1,645 billionaires in the world, "with an aggregate net worth of $6.4 trillion." You know what that number looks like. There are 172 women billionaires, up from 138 last year. A net worth of $31 billion was needed to make the top 20, up from $23 billion last year. The US had the most billionaires: 492. China followed with 152, and then Russia with 111.

Microsoft cofounder Bill Gates, fifty-eight years old, topped the list with an estimated net worth of $76 billion. As of May 16, 2013, Gates had donated $28 billion to the Bill and Melinda Gates Foundation, established "globally, to enhance healthcare and reduce extreme poverty, and in America, to expand educational opportunities and access to information technology."

Facebook's Mark Zuckerberg, age 29, was "the biggest gainer in 2013, with his fortune jumping $15.2 billion to $28.5 billion." Reports are that Zuckerberg and his wife, Priscilla Chan, were the most generous American philanthropists in 2013. They contributed 18 million Facebook shares worth $990 million to the Silicon Valley Community Foundation, which its website says exists to "build and energize a community of philanthropists who strengthen the common good."

If you or I had anywhere near that level of wealth, we might choose charitable recipients quite different from those noted above. There are many charitable endeavors with both temporal and eternal impact. They are worthy of our generous support!

Six truths come to mind from these two reports:

1. Many people in the world live in abject poverty. A few possess unimaginable wealth.

2. Everything we have comes from God and really belongs to Him, not to us (1 Chronicles 29:11, 14).

3. "We brought nothing into the world, and we cannot take anything out of the world" (1 Timothy 6:7).

4. We are simply managers of whatever God entrusts to our care (Matthew 25:14–30).

5. Jesus tells us to feed the hungry and to clothe the naked (Matthew 25:31–46).

6. He also says, "Everyone to whom much . . . [is] given, of him much will be required" (Luke 12:48).

Some of the world's wealthiest understand these truths. Others probably have no clue. The same could be said of most of us whose wealth is measured not in trillions but in other treasures from our heavenly Father's bountiful hand. Some of us understand our privilege and responsibility. Others don't. May God help us to increase the numbers of those who do!

Freedom!

VOLUME V, NUMBER 46—JULY 3, 2014

Tomorrow is the Fourth of July, a celebration of the signing of the Declaration of Independence from Great Britain. Adopted on July 4, 1776, by the Continental Congress, the Declaration announced that the thirteen American colonies, then at war with Great Britain, regarded themselves as thirteen newly independent sovereign states and no longer a part of the British Empire. Instead, they formed a new nation—the United States of America.

For many Americans, tomorrow will simply be another holiday, a time to stay home from work and perhaps to gather with family and friends around BBQ and other festivities. For all of us, it should be a time of remembrance and appreciation for the decision of our country's forefathers to establish a nation that would be free to determine its own destiny.

Freedom is often taken for granted. Only when it is threatened do we fully appreciate its intrinsic value. That's true in the personal, professional, political, and religious aspects of life. No individuals or groups of people thrive under domineering, self-serving, controlling leadership. And when that type of leadership evolves, it's just a matter of time before those living under oppression make the kinds of decisions that precipitated the Declaration of Independence.

The words of St. Paul are worth remembering: "For freedom Christ has set us free; stand firm therefore, and do not submit again to a yoke of slavery" (Galatians 5:1).

Many blessings to you this special day!

Nine-Eleven XIII

VOLUME VI, NUMBER 4—SEPTEMBER 11, 2014

Today is the thirteenth anniversary of the terrorism in 2001 that ended the lives of over three thousand innocent Americans at the World Trade Center in New York City, the Pentagon in Washington, DC, and a field in Pennsylvania. That day, now known simply as 9/11, radically changed life in America and the world. A succinct report of 9/11 is available at http://www.history.com/topics/9-11-attacks.

The perpetrators were identified as members of al-Qaeda, an Islamic terrorist group. Their activity in different parts of the world has ebbed and flowed these past thirteen years. Al-Qaeda is not as frequently mentioned today as another emerging and even more violent jihadist group known as the Islamic State of Iraq and Syria (ISIS). Both groups are demonic.

Many of us recall clearly where we were and what we were doing that Tuesday morning thirteen years ago. Not so with others. Today's university students were barely old enough to remember 9/11. Current elementary and junior high students were not yet born. Some who in 2001 were already advanced in age have passed away, and others have lost those memories.

The original 9/11 was a traumatic day for our nation. More such days may lie ahead. What to do?

- Pray that God will thwart terrorists in order that such dastardly deeds do not reoccur.

- Vote and pray for leaders who are willing to confront evil of every kind, preferably as part of a multinational coalition against terrorism, or unilaterally if necessary.

- Pray for and support our military personnel who serve and sacrifice at great cost.

- Pray this prayer of Solomon: "If Your people go out to battle against their enemy . . . and they pray to the LORD . . . , then hear in heaven their prayer and their plea" (1 Kings 8:44, 45).

- Remember this truth: "The eternal God is your dwelling place, and underneath are the everlasting arms" (Deuteronomy 33:27).

May the remembrance of the atrocities of September 11, 2001, move the people and leaders of our nation and world to greater trust in the providence and protection of almighty God and increased determination to work toward living in peace in the face of evil.

Isaiah says it well:

> Come, let us go up to the mountain of the LORD . . . that He
> may teach us His ways and that we may walk in His paths.
> . . . He shall judge between the nations, . . . and they shall
> beat their swords into plowshares, and their spears into
> pruning hooks; nation shall not lift up sword against nation,
> neither shall they learn war anymore. (Isaiah 2:3, 4)

Lord, hasten that day!

Christian Persecution

VOLUME VI, NUMBER 6—SEPTEMBER 25, 2014

My first awareness of Christian persecution was in the 1951 movie *Quo Vadis*. Filmed by MGM in Technicolor, the movie was based on an 1896 novel of the same title by Henryk Sienkiewicz.

One of my sisters and I saw that movie together. She was eleven, and I was eight. We probably had other schoolmates with us, but I don't recall that detail. The movie featured actors and actresses (that's what we called female actors in those days) whose names meant nothing to me at the time. The list included Robert Taylor, Deborah Kerr, Peter Ustinov, and Sophia Loren.

My primary recollection from that movie is the shock of seeing the portrayal of early Christians defenselessly and brutally attacked by roaring, raging lions in an arena, most likely the Roman Colosseum. That unthinkable act was ordered by Nero, who became emperor of Rome at age 17 and held that title from AD 54 till AD 68. It was during his rule that Rome burned (AD 64) and the stage was set for the destruction of the temple in Jerusalem (AD 70).

Christian persecution continues today. According to Open Doors, an organization with the tag line, "Serving persecuted Christians worldwide," (https://www.opendoorsusa.org/christian-persecution/), "Christians are the most persecuted religious group worldwide. An average of at least 180 Christians around the world are killed each month for their faith."

At least four thoughts come to mind:

1. Deep concern and heartfelt prayer for Christians living under persecution.

2. Thankfulness for the blessing of living in a country relatively free from that scourge.

3. Encouragement for all who read these words to exercise the privilege and responsibility of electing leaders at every level

who take seriously the growing threat of Christian persecution and its undeniable consequences in the world, including in our own country.

4. "Bad men need nothing more to compass their ends, than that good men should look on and do nothing" (John Stuart Mill).

Carpe diem!

63

Living Generously

Volume VI, Number 7—October 2, 2014

That's the focus of the current sermon and Bible class series at Zion Lutheran Church in Walburg, Texas, the congregation to which Terry and I belong. Senior Pastor John Davenport and new Associate Pastor Kevin Hintze are ably leading the congregation in a sensitive yet direct exploration of the relationship between people, possessions, and the God to whom they belong.

Some of us discovered that relationship long ago, thanks to parents, grandparents, pastors, teachers, or other significant people in our lives who taught us that though in many ways we are richly blessed, those blessings do not really belong to us. They are not possessions we own but treasures entrusted to our care by the generous and gracious hand of God.

Occasionally, even those of us who know that truth need a gentle reminder. It's so easy to forget, especially when times are good and financial resources are plentiful.

But when times are tough and adversity strikes, the things in life that we value so highly quickly become less important, replaced by the significant realities that truly matter. That includes faith, family, forgiveness, health, home, and heaven.

Jesus said: "Do not be anxious. . . . Your heavenly Father knows that you need . . . all [these things]. But seek first the kingdom of God and His righteousness, and all these things will be added to you" (Matthew 6:31, 32–33).

And St. Paul wrote: "He who supplies seed to the sower and bread for food will supply and multiply your seed for sowing and increase the harvest of your righteousness. You will be enriched in every way to be generous in every way" (2 Corinthians 9:10–11).

With that promise on your mind and in your heart, live generously!

A Little Girl Named Katelyn

VOLUME VI, NUMBER 11—OCTOBER 23, 2014

This past weekend, Terry and I joined the celebration of the sixtieth anniversary of Pilgrim Lutheran School in Houston. In 1966, I taught fourth grade there for four months, filling in for a young mother on maternity leave. My classroom duties began three days after our wedding and ended days before we moved to Springfield, Illinois, for me to attend Concordia Theological Seminary.

During the Sunday service, I noticed across the aisle a little girl who was crying while the offering was being gathered. Looking more closely, I detected a coin in her little clenched hand. About that time, she looked toward the back of the sanctuary at the ushers who were making their way from the back to the front. I deduced that she was deeply upset about missing the offering plate.

Her mother was saying something to her that was impossible for me to hear. But I surmised that Mom had suggested her daughter could still deposit her offering since the ushers would pass by again on their way to the front of the sanctuary to place the offering plates on the altar. Unaware of the dilemma, the ushers walked right past her pew, which catalyzed additional tears.

After briefly pondering if and how it would be appropriate to help, I quickly got out of my seat, walked across the aisle, knelt beside the little girl, and asked her mother if the little girl was crying because she missed the offering. Mom's answer was in the affirmative. So I asked the mother if it would be okay for her daughter to go with me to the altar to put her offering in the plate. She readily agreed. So did the little girl, whose sadness suddenly turned to satisfaction.

Hand in hand, a little girl and a man she had never met walked down the center aisle and up the chancel steps. When we stood at the altar, which was much too tall for her to reach, I asked if I could pick her up so she could reach the plate. She nodded in agreement. I picked her up, she completed her mission, and we walked back together to her appreciative mother. On the way, I noticed no small number of smiling worshipers who had witnessed what had transpired.

Although I didn't know it at the time, I learned from her mother after the service that the little girl's name is Katelyn. She is four years old. When I saw the coin she placed in the plate, I was reminded of the biblical story of the widow who gave all she had. And I was thankful that I did not let my initial concern about possibly making a scene or interfering in a parental matter prevent me from taking what turned out to be a most rewarding risk.

Paul's Missionary Journeys

VOLUME VI, NUMBER 14—NOVEMBER 13, 2014

Terry and I just returned from an eleven-day trip to Turkey and Greece during which I served as lecturer on the missionary journeys of the apostle Paul. We sailed from Istanbul to Athens, with stops in Troy/ Troas, Sardis/Ephesus, Kos, Rhodes, Laodicea/ Hierapolis, Santorini, and Corinth.

In most of these ancient cities, ruins have been excavated sufficiently to enable identification of homes, businesses, civic buildings, temples, and churches. Amazing architecture and incredible construction techniques produced structures beyond comprehension. In some cases, gigantic stone blocks weighing many tons rested for centuries atop mammoth stone pillars.

The New Testament contains information about Paul's three separate missionary journeys, probably conducted between AD 45 and 58. Each was several years in length. During these trips, Paul preached the news of Jesus in many important coastal cities and trade route towns.

God used Paul's ministry to bring the Gospel to the Gentiles, establishing the Christian Church in places beyond its point of origin. Paul was aided by Barnabas, John Mark, Silas, Luke, and Timothy. Positively received by many, Paul and his message were rejected by others who expressed their disapproval by beating him, stoning him, imprisoning him, and running him out of town.

Because of his bold testimony of Jesus, Saul the persecutor became Paul the persecuted.

Although Paul's missionary journeys caused him to sacrifice everything, he said his sufferings were worth the cost: "I count everything as loss because of the surpassing worth of knowing Christ Jesus my Lord. For His sake I have suffered the loss of all things and count them as rubbish, in order that I may gain Christ and be found in Him" (Philippians 3:8–9).

Last week's journey greatly enhanced our appreciation for Paul and his courageous ministry! I hope you share that appreciation!

Giving Thanks for People and Other Blessings

Volume VI, Number 16—November 27, 2014

If you haven't done so in a while, I recommend making a list on this Thanksgiving Day of the people and other blessings for whom and for which you are most thankful. It's a fairly safe guess that most of our lists would include some or all of the following:

People:
- Parents
- Spouse
- Children
- Grandchildren
- Siblings
- Pastors
- Teachers
- Friends
- Neighbors
- Public servants
- Health-care providers
- Police and fire men and women
- Military service men and women

Blessings:
- Health
- Home
- Food
- Faith
- Freedom
- Forgiveness
- Peace
- Prosperity
- Safety
- Security
- Vocation
- Employment
- Income and financial resources

Perhaps this outline will be helpful in preparing your own list. Where possible, be specific. Fill in the blanks. Name the family members and friends for whom you are thankful, and let them know they made your list.

This Thanksgiving, take some time to thank God for these very important people and blessings!

"Oh give thanks to the LORD, for He is good, for His steadfast love endures forever!" (Psalm 106:1).

Leaving This World . . . Slowly or Suddenly

VOLUME VI, NUMBER 22—JANUARY 8, 2015

Last month, I visited a longtime friend and co-worker, Dr. Keith Loomans, who is at home under hospice care, spending what appear to be his last days on this earth. His wife, Margie, and other family members are lovingly caring for Keith, trying to make him as comfortable as possible, even though he struggles valiantly for every breath of life.

Conversely, during the recent holidays, I received word of the sudden death of two LCMS clergy friends of mine. Rev. Dr. Ronald Fink, former parish pastor and past LCMS Atlantic District President, died suddenly December 27 at the age of seventy-seven after preaching two days earlier at a Christmas Eve service. Terry and I traveled with Ron and his wife, Millie, on our recent cruise following the footsteps of the apostle Paul. Ron appeared healthy and was doing just fine on our trip. Apparently, he suffered a heart attack or stroke or aneurysm that took his life instantly.

Rev. Kim DeVries, longtime pastor of Mount Calvary Lutheran Church in San Antonio, passed away New Year's Day. He was not yet sixty-five years old and apparently suffered a heart attack or blood clot while jogging. Terry and I were with Kim and his wife, Cathy, in November at the LCEF Fall Conference in California. Though seemingly in excellent health, Kim died suddenly. He leaves Cathy, two sons, their wives, two grandsons, and other family members to mourn his passing.

People who lose loved ones as the result of lengthy illness have the burden of walking with their loved one through the valley of the shadow of death. They see and are deeply saddened by the pain and suffering their loved ones experience, often resulting from medical treatments intended to cure the disease that has captured the loved one's being.

People who lose loved ones to sudden, unexpected death are shocked by the loss and the unhappy experience of not being able to say goodbye or to prepare themselves in advance. If the loved one is taken prematurely, there's a sense of regret or remorse that the expected longevity of the loved one in question was abbreviated. There may also be feelings of anger at being cheated and robbed of future time and life experiences that have suddenly and irreversibly vanished.

There's no easy way to lose a loved one, whether he or she leaves this world slowly or suddenly. Although it's not a frequent topic of conversation, and while I'm certainly not in any rush, I've told Terry that should the Lord choose to take me quickly, may His holy name be praised!

Either way, as the hymn says, for all of us: "I'm but a stranger here, Heav'n is my home" (*LSB* 748:1).

The Public Baptism of an Unwed Mother's Child

Volume VI, Number 23—January 15, 2015

Recently while traveling, Terry and I worshiped at a congregation of our church body. That's a common practice for us when we're away from home. That Sunday morning, we experienced something that's not very common at all: the public Baptism of an unwed mother's child.

We later learned that this young lady of seventeen years had left home at sixteen, had become pregnant, and had subsequently returned home. After giving birth to her baby, with support from her family and pastor, she decided to have her baby baptized on Sunday morning in a public worship service rather than in a private service at a different day and time.

As I watched this young lady, who is younger than both of our university-student grandchildren, I wondered what her life as a very young single mother would be like in the years ahead. How does a teenage mother support herself and her child? How does she deal with the judgmental attitude of friends and acquaintances? How does she pick up the pieces of a broken heart and spirit most likely resulting from a severed relationship with the father of her newborn child?

I know of other similar situations where the parents of a young unwed mother have openly embraced their daughter and her child, lovingly providing emotional, financial, and spiritual support for both. While acknowledging the moral mistake that led to the reality they faced, they wisely knew that to forsake or abandon their daughter and grandchild would essentially constitute responding to one wrongful act with wrongful acts of their own. Thankfully for all concerned, they chose to emulate the actions of the father of the prodigal son in Holy Scripture and to receive mother and child with open arms and forgiving hearts.

What struck me most about our experience that Sunday morning was the courage of the young mother to request the Baptism of her child in a public rather than private worship service. That decision was particularly poignant in light of the fact that, years ago, young women in identical situations were required to endure the shame of personally standing before their Christian congregation, embarrassingly admitting their sin and receiving public chastisement for their wrongdoing before, at least in some cases, obtaining corporate forgiveness.

The young mother we saw had received forgiveness from pastor and parents. With their support, she made the right decision not to terminate her pregnancy but to give birth to the life within her womb. She then chose to bring her baby to the waters of Holy Baptism in a public worship service.

There, in the presence of her fellow Christians, she quietly yet openly demonstrated a truth all of us would do well to remember and replicate. When we sin, which we do every day, we ask for and receive God's forgiveness. Then we move forward in life, doing everything we can as forgiven children of God to transform the result of sin into a manifestation of the grace of God within us.

Terry and I were powerfully blessed by this young lady's example of doing just that!

Forty-Nine Years Ago

VOLUME VI, NUMBER 25—JANUARY 29, 2015

It was a cold January 29 in central Texas. The temperature in Austin that night reached 12 degrees. Thankfully, Terry and I were able to spend the night at the Stagecoach Inn in Salado and not in a tent or on the parking lot!

The weekend of our wedding began Friday evening with the rehearsal at St. Paul Lutheran Church in Austin, the congregation of Terry's birth, Baptism, and confirmation. It was the obvious venue for our matrimonial vows.

St. Paul also operated the school at which I had taught thirty fourth graders the year before. I had been hired for that position August 15, 1964, fresh out of Texas A&M with a degree in Animal Science, for the princely sum of two hundred dollars per month. For a few days, I thought I must have really impressed Pastor Albert Jesse, who hired me on the spot. Then it occurred to me that school would be starting only two weeks later, and he desperately needed a teacher in that classroom!

After the rehearsal dinner, I kissed Terry goodnight Friday at midnight, drove the one hundred miles back to College Station and got to bed shortly after 2:00 a.m. Saturday. My last graduate school final for that semester was biochemistry at 7:00 a.m. You can probably guess my score on that exam! Not all that great, mostly because my mind and heart were focused elsewhere.

The grad school idea came after one year of fourth-grade teaching. I was persuaded that church work would be my vocational ambition but that, most likely, the elementary classroom would not be my final destination. A master's degree in biology would open additional opportunities. That plan was never completed, replaced with a decision to go to the seminary instead.

After the final was finished, I got in my '57 Chevy with all my worldly goods and drove back to Austin. The short afternoon was spent "hanging out" with Mom, Dad, and my three sisters. Wedding participants had been instructed by Pastor Jesse to be at St. Paul shortly after 3:00 p.m. That was a good thing, since my best man had forgotten to pick up Terry's rings.

The worship and wedding service was wonderful, meaningful, and memorable. Pastor Jesse's sermon was based on John 2, the first miracle of Jesus at the wedding at Cana in Galilee. The title was "They Invited Jesus to the Wedding!"

After the service and photo session, we went to the reception at the Villa Capri Hotel in Austin, which no longer exists. It was picture perfect. Not extravagant, just very nice. On the way to our two-night honeymoon stay in Salado, Terry asked what I thought of the groom's cake. My reply: "What groom's cake?" I hadn't even seen it or known it was there.

We spent Saturday and Sunday nights at the Stagecoach Inn, which at twenty dollars per night pretty much blew our meager budget. Monday morning we drove back to Austin, picked up Terry's belongings and our wedding gifts, and drove to our first apartment in Houston, a clean but not at all fancy one-bedroom apartment that we rented for seventy-five dollars per month. We paid half every two weeks.

The next morning, I was in another fourth-grade classroom, teaching one semester at Pilgrim Lutheran School in Houston for a teacher who was on maternity leave that semester. Four months later, we moved to Springfield, Illinois, then the home of Concordia Theological Seminary. It might just as well have been the end of the world as far as our parents were concerned.

All that and everything that followed had its official beginning forty-nine years ago today. Lots of water has gone under our bridge since then, most of it joyful, some of it stressful. Through it all, we have relied on our love for each other and God's grace. We will continue to do so, as we pledged that January night in cold central Texas, "until death parts us, according to God's holy will."

Happy anniversary, dear Terry! I love you with all my heart!

Biblical Ethics for Electronic Blogging

VOLUME VI, NUMBER 26—FEBRUARY 5, 2015

Several months ago, a friend and colleague of mine, at my request, offered a few suggested topics for me to consider writing about. Today's topic is one of his suggestions.

Suggestions like this are not made in a vacuum but on the basis of personal experience. I'm quite certain that such is the case with my friend and his recommendation.

Electronic blogging, practically defined, is anything a person writes or posts on the internet on a regular or irregular basis. Some consider my Perspectives articles to be blogs, which is okay with me.

The problem arises when a blogger (the author of the blog) violates the will of God, especially the Eighth Commandment: "Thou shalt not bear false witness against thy neighbour" (Exodus 20:16 KJV). Newer versions say: "You shall not give false testimony against your neighbor" (Exodus 20:16 NIV). In both cases, the meaning is the same and sets a biblical ethical standard for any kind of communication.

The catechism's explanation of this commandment says: "We should fear and love God so that we do not tell lies about our neighbor, betray him, slander him, or hurt his reputation, but defend him, speak well of him, and explain everything in the kindest way" (Small Catechism, explanation of the Eighth Commandment). An older version uses slightly different words, adding the injunction to "put the best construction on everything" (*Concordia Triglotta,* explanation of the Eighth Commandment).

There are blogs written by people who claim to be Christian, even some who belong to our own Lutheran Church—Missouri Synod, including pastors on the LCMS clergy roster, that fall far short of this standard. Self-justification for judgmental and caustic characterizations is based on insistence that their interpretation of the topic at hand is the only correct and orthodox one and that anyone who disagrees with their way of looking at the matter is dead wrong.

There's nothing wrong with expressing respectful and even strong disagreement with someone else's understanding of what the Bible says (or doesn't say) about a particular matter of faith and life. The problem is that some bloggers don't stop there but continue with ad hominem personal attacks against the one(s) with whom they disagree. Some get downright nasty and vulgar!

Bloggers fall far short of putting the best construction on everything when they do just the opposite of what the Eighth Commandment commands. By jumping to and writing judgmental conclusions about the person with whom they disagree, they often betray, slander, and hurt the other person's reputation rather than defending and speaking well of him or her.

The Bible says: "In your hearts honor Christ the Lord as holy, always being prepared to make a defense to anyone who asks you for a reason for the hope that is in you; yet do it with gentleness and respect" (1 Peter 3:15). That's a biblical ethic for any kind of communication, including electronic blogging!

God's Presence in Your Life

VOLUME VI, NUMBER 30—MARCH 5, 2015

One of the most profound questions I frequently hear people asking goes something like this: "If there is a God, does He really know who I am, and does He really care about my life?"

As a Christian person, husband, father, grandfather, pastor, theologian, ecclesiastical supervisor, former regional and national church body leader, and current Concordia University presidential ambassador, my answer is this: Absolutely yes!

It may seem God is absent from our lives in times of personal difficulty or national disaster. But the Bible says God is always with us. He knows how many hairs we have on our head (Matthew 10:30). Nothing in all creation can separate us from His love, not even death (Romans 8:35–39).

A few years ago, LCMS Eastern District President Chris Wicher shared with me a story that some might dismiss as mere coincidence. I think it illustrates God's presence and activity in our lives.

Chris and a few pastors and other men were driving around the flooded area of Pittston, Pennsylvania, looking for people who needed help in cleaning up their flooded homes. They came to a couple standing in front of their home, simply staring at the damage. The car stopped, and one of the pastors asked if they needed help.

The people responded, "No, not really. We don't know where to begin, and besides the house does not yet have electricity restored."

The would-be helpers told who they were and that they were driving around to see if they could be of help. They told the couple, "We have a generator, pump, mops, buckets, and Clorox."

Quite moved by this generous offer, the homeowners accepted the help, and in a few hours, the cleanup was completed. But that's not all. Not five minutes before the carload of generous helpers offered their assistance, the couple had prayed to the Lord for direction and help! I would submit that God answered their prayer by sending some very good-hearted men to their door.

The love of Jesus moves people to acts of kindness. Such kindness demonstrates, in this and in many other circumstances, the presence and care of God in the lives of His people.

Important Questions

VOLUME VI, NUMBER 32—MARCH 19, 2015

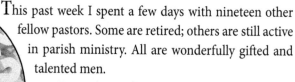

This past week I spent a few days with nineteen other fellow pastors. Some are retired; others are still active in parish ministry. All are wonderfully gifted and talented men.

During one of our sessions, the leader asked those of us who are no longer active in congregational ministry a number of important questions:

1. What's a Bible passage that means a lot to you?

2. What attribute of God is most important to you?

3. What's going on in your life that is significant?

4. What's a question you would like to ask the rest of us or anyone else, perhaps even God?

5. What's an insight you would like to share with the group or with someone else?

The ensuing conversation was awesome! The seven of us in that group had a combined total of 317 years in ministerial leadership of one kind or another. That's an average of over 45 years each! We all shared heartfelt matters, not the least of which is the desire to "finish well."

In a subsequent conversation, it was clear that finishing well referred not simply to vocational retirement per se. It was mostly about doing whatever it takes to influence for Christ as many people as possible, especially family members and nonbelievers, as long as we're alive.

Regardless of your current age, vocation, experience, or personal or family circumstances, I encourage you to contemplate those same important questions. They very well might have the same impact on you that they had on seven chronologically mature clergymen last week!

Spring Break and Holy Week

VOLUME VI, NUMBER 34—APRIL 2, 2015

Both spring break and Holy Week attract millions of people annually. That's where the similarity ends. Consider the following differences and disparities between the two.

Several newspaper and TV reports this week have focused in a graphic way on recent spring break activities. Video clips have shown raucous and even lewd behavior of young people by themselves or in small groups in the midst of huge crowds of barely clothed humanity.

In almost every case, mass consumption of alcohol is involved. One method of such volumetric booze delivery is a beer-filled plastic funnel attached to a tube that goes straight into the mouth of the consumer. Another shows scantily clad young women and men chug-a-lugging gin or vodka straight from the bottle. Other methods might be both more creative and destructive.

Tragically, those reports include news of seven young people being shot last weekend in Panama City Beach, Florida. During February and March, up to six million young people visit that small town of twelve thousand, which has been dubbed "the Spring Break Capital of the World."

Other reports are of young spring breakers who have died from excessive alcohol consumption or drug abuse. Contributing factors include a large number of underage drinkers and widespread availability of heroin, together with an increasingly popular club drug called Molly.

Contrast that dangerous and deadly scenario with the meditative, reflective, penitential mood of Holy Week. Celebrated by billions of Christians worldwide, this week's events include Maundy Thursday, Good Friday, Holy Saturday, and Easter Sunday—the Festival of the Resurrection.

Scripture and worship throughout this week will focus on the Passion of Christ, including

- the Passover in the Upper Room, with Jesus initiating the Lord's Supper;

- the suffering and arrest of Jesus in the Garden of Gethsemane;

- His trial and sentence of death before Roman authorities;

- His crucifixion on a hill named Calvary, also called "the place of the skull";

- His embalming by faithful women and burial in a borrowed tomb; and

- His miraculous resurrection from that grave three days later!

Spring break focuses on the unchecked and uninhibited natural inclination of mankind toward self-gratification. Holy Week's emphasis is the sacrificial act of Christ for the forgiveness of humanity's self-centered failure to live life according to the purpose for which God created us.

Terry and I join each of you, especially this Holy Week, in thanking God for His Son, Jesus! Soon we'll all be saying: "Christ is risen! He is risen indeed!"

Five Things Your Kids Will Remember about You

VOLUME VI, NUMBER 37—APRIL 23, 2015

This past week I came across an article by Dave Willis titled "The Five Things Your Kids Will Remember about You" (www.patheos.com/blogs/davewillis/the-5-things-your-kids-will-remember-about-you/). The article was followed by encouragement to share it with others.

As parents, we tend to stress about things that don't matter all that much. Our kids probably aren't going to remember every detail of our home décor, or how perfect our landscaping looked or whether our refrigerator was stocked with name brands or generics. Let's focus on what really matters. If you want to know what your kids will remember about you, here it is:

1. The times you made them feel safe (or the times you made them feel unsafe).

There's a vulnerability and a need for protection in the heart of every child. Your kids will remember those moments you chased the monsters from under their bed or held them after a nightmare, but they'll also remember the times your temper became the monster they feared. Our kids are probably going to see us angry sometimes, because that's part of life, but make it your mission to make your children feel safe and secure at all times when they're with you.

2. The times you gave them your undivided attention.

Kids measure love primarily by our attentiveness to them. The times you stop what you're doing to have a tea party or go outside to throw a ball or jump on a trampoline . . . [will] be memories etched into their minds and hearts forever. Take the time to do the little things with your kids, because in the end, they'll be the moments that matter most.

3. The way you interacted with your spouse.

Our kids are forming their views of love in large part by watching how we treat our husband or wife. Strive to have the kind of marriage that makes them excited to get married someday. Give them the security that comes from seeing their Mom and Dad in a committed, loving relationship with each other.

4. Your words of affirmation AND your words of criticism.

A child's heart is like wet cement and the impression made early in life will harden over time. They'll base their sense of identity, capability and even self-worth largely upon the words you speak to them in those formative years. Part of our job as parents is to correct and discipline, but even in correction, let your words be full of love, encouragement and positive reinforcement.

5. Your family traditions.

Kids love spontaneity, but they also have deep need for predictability. They'll remember with great fondness the "traditions" you establish whether it's a weekly family movie (or game) night, a place you regularly travel for family getaways, the way you celebrate birthdays and special events or any other special tradition. Be intentional about creating some traditions that they'll want to pass on to their own children someday.

While not specifically mentioned in the article, you and I would surely want to amplify this list, perhaps in the family traditions category, by adding items near and dear to our Christian heart. Examples might include reading Bible stories to our children and teaching them to pray, to worship, to sing, to share, to forgive, and to have compassion on the needy, the lonely, the outcast.

This will hopefully be helpful to you and your family. Many blessings!

More Thoughts on Fatherly Influence

VOLUME VI, NUMBER 49—JULY 9, 2015

Wouldn't it be great if every person born into this world would be blessed with a positive paternal experience? Sadly, that's simply not the reality.

By the grace of God, some do just fine in life without the influence of a mature, responsible, godly father. In other cases, the absence of positive male parental guidance results in disrespect for authority and lack of development of proper boundaries. Not infrequently in such cases, life with minimal meaning, purpose, or productivity, or something much worse, is the end result.

This topic has been researched for years. Some have come to the conclusion that there may very well be a connection between a positive male role model and the development of self-control and other appropriate behaviors. Compared to children raised in two-parent homes, children who grow up in the absence of their father are often not nearly as well-balanced and responsible.

What's the bottom line? Consider these encouragements:

If you are blessed with a father who was or still is a positive role model for you of what it means to be a Christian person, especially expressing unequivocal love, care, guidance, and direction in your life, thank God for that wonderful blessing!

If that blessed man is still alive, let him know how much his influence has meant to you. A phone call, handwritten note, email, or text message will make his day!

If you are a father, do not underestimate the importance of your presence, attention, and guidance in the life of your child, regardless of his or her age. A loving, caring, affirming, encouraging, godly father and mother are the most important people in a person's life.

Speaking of mothers, if you are a father, do not underestimate the lasting impression on your child made by the way you love, respect, and cherish your wife. Especially in relationships between husbands and wives, actions speak louder than words!

In relating both to spouses and to children, remember the adage: Wives and children spell love T-I-M-E!

It's my prayer that your life has been molded and shaped by a positive paternal experience. If so, join me in thanking God for the lifelong influence of a good and godly father! If that's not the case, don't hesitate to let me know. Perhaps I can help.

Have Courage! Be Kind!

VOLUME VI, NUMBER 50—JULY 16, 2015

There's a very inexpensive movie theater fairly near our home. Tickets are $2.00 each. For seniors, they're $1.50. Sweet! On Wednesdays, seniors get in for $1.00. Even sweeter!

Understandably, newly released movies don't show up on the marquee right away. That's okay. For that price, a guy like me who was raised during pretty tough economic times can wait.

So occasionally, when something interesting is being shown, I'll meet Terry on my way home from my work day at Concordia University Texas. We'll go to a late afternoon matinee, followed by a shared entrée at Hunan Lion, our favorite oriental restaurant.

Movie and dinner for two: under $20. Time together with my wife of nearly fifty years: priceless!

Last week we saw the version of *Cinderella* that was released this year. It wasn't really in the same category as my favorites, like Indiana Jones or James Bond. But watching it was time well spent. Actually, it was a wonderful movie!

It's probably not necessary to review here the plot of this classic fairytale. Suffice it to say that the story portrays a mixture of the power of parental love, the pain of dysfunctional blended family abuse, and the pleasure of romantic fantasy becoming reality.

Along with memorable scenes and remarkable animation, one of the most powerful highlights was the deathbed dialogue between Ella (later derogatorily named Cinderella by her evil stepsisters) and her biological mother. Mother asked daughter to forgive her for leaving so soon by dying. Ella obliged. Then mother advised daughter: "Have courage! Be kind!"

Good advice that Cinderella followed consistently. That included her parting words, late in the story, to her cruel stepmother, Lady Tremaine: "I forgive you." Regardless of the reason for the pronouncement, in any context those words require both courage and kindness.

The Old Testament relates the advice of Moses to Joshua: "Be strong and courageous" (Deuteronomy 31:7). That encouragement was followed by this promise: "It is the Lord who goes before you. He will be with you; He will not leave you or forsake you. Do not fear or be dismayed" (Deuteronomy 31:8)

Paul writes to the Ephesians: "Be kind to one another, tenderhearted, forgiving one another, as God in Christ forgave you" (Ephesians 4:32)

Have courage! Be kind! Those wise and biblically based words for living are worth heeding. Even when the reminder to do so comes from a fairytale!

Fifty Years Together

VOLUME VII, NUMBER 27—JANUARY 28, 2016

Terry and I were married at St. Paul Lutheran Church at 5:00 p.m. on January 29, 1966. Her childhood pastor, Rev. Albert Jesse, based his homily on the miracle of Jesus changing water into wine at a wedding in Cana of Galilee. His homily was titled, "They Invited Jesus to the Wedding."

At the reception at the Villa Capri Hotel, I was so excited I failed to see the groom's cake, a fine southern tradition. After the reception we drove in my two-door, baby blue '65 Chevy Malibu (which had replaced my worn out '57 Chevy) sixty miles north to Salado, spending our two-night honeymoon at the Stagecoach Inn. The honeymoon suite was twenty dollars per night, a significant expenditure fifty years ago, especially on a salary of two hundred dollars per month.

Lots of water has gone under the bridge since then. During our fifty years together, Terry has been at my side providing love, patience, support, and partnership. Our ministry has included

- three years at Concordia Theological Seminary in Springfield, Illinois;

- one year of pastoral internship at Ascension Lutheran Church in Charlotte, North Carolina;

- three years of pastoral ministry at Good Shepherd Lutheran Church in Biloxi, Mississippi;

- eight years of pastoral ministry at Redeemer Lutheran Church in Beaumont, Texas;

- five years of mission development at Faith Lutheran Church in Georgetown, Texas;

- five years of planned giving with Lutheran Foundation of Texas in Austin, Texas;

- ten years as president of the Texas District of the LCMS in Austin, Texas;

- nine years as president of The Lutheran Church—Missouri Synod in St. Louis, Missouri;

- five years as Presidential Ambassador at Concordia University Texas in Austin, Texas;

- one month back at Lutheran Foundation of Texas as Inheritance Legacy Consultant.

In each of these places of ministry, Terry's unique gifts of hospitality and encouragement have provided support, comfort, hope, and joy for wives of countless pastors, ecclesiastical supervisors, and other regional, national, and international church leaders. Noncatered seated dinners with scores of guests in our homes in Georgetown, Round Rock, and St. Louis were not uncommon.

In addition, beginning with our mission development days in Georgetown, Terry helped support our family by going back to work. She spent several years at a women's clothing store in Georgetown, followed by seventeen years of six-days-a-week employment in the wholesale fine jewelry business.

Both of us have been blessed with loving parents and grandparents, only one of whom is still living—my 99¾-year-old mother, Elda, of New Braunfels, Texas. We have also been blessed with our daughter, Angie; her husband, Todd (Terry calls him our son-in-love); their children (our grandchildren), Kolby and Kayla; and our son, Andrew.

We are very thankful for Terry's brother; my three sisters; my sisters' spouses, children, and grandchildren; and our aunts, uncles, cousins, nieces, and nephews. We're also wonderfully blessed with countless friends and colleagues from across the nation and around the world, including many of you.

When asked what I believe are the most important words in a successful marriage, I usually say "Yes, dear!" Seriously, more important words are "I love you!" "I'm sorry!" "I forgive you!"

As most married couples will attest, marriage is a mixture of good days and bad, happy times and sad. While it's incredible how much alike Terry and I often think, it's equally incredible that each of us will still sometimes say or do things that cause the other to raise an eyebrow or shake a head in surprise, amazement, or even frustration.

What's the bottom line? I give thanks, honor, and glory to God for half a century of joy and sorrow, blessing and difficulty, victory and defeat, under the umbrella of God's grace with Terry at my side. She has many gifts and unselfishly uses them joyfully and generously.

Fifty years ago, the words each of us spoke to the other included "I take you to be my wedded spouse, to have and to hold from this day forward, for better, for worse, for richer, for poorer, in sickness and in health, to love, to honor, and to cherish, till death parts us, according to God's holy will." By God's grace, we said what we meant and meant what we said. To God be the glory!

Resurrection!

VOLUME VII, NUMBER 35—MARCH 24, 2016

This is the week before Easter, aka the Festival of the Resurrection of Our Lord. It's a busy time for most pastors, who are heavily involved in preparation for special Holy Week observations of the Paschal Triduum. That's one name for the three-day period from Maundy Thursday evening through Good Friday and Holy Saturday and until Easter Sunday evening.

In Western Christianity, Easter is always the Sunday after the full moon that occurs on or after the spring equinox on March 21. Easter can come as early as March 22 or as late as April 25.

Regardless of its date, I've always been amazed by the Festival of the Resurrection, which observes Jesus' coming back to life. What a miracle! No one can prove it actually occurred. Nor can anyone disprove it. I don't understand it. It's a matter of faith. The Bible says it. I believe it.

We Christians confess in the Third Article of the Apostles' Creed: "I believe in . . . the resurrection of the body, and the life everlasting." We believe not only that Jesus came back to life but also that we will do the same. Every time I speak those words, I'm saying I believe that someday a miracle will occur, transforming my dead body back to life again.

Last week, Terry and I went to Houston for the memorial service of my youngest sister's mother-in-law. On the way back to Georgetown via New Braunfels to see my mother, we visited my father's grave site. His physical body has been in that grave for more than one third of a century. The thought that what's left in that casket will come back to life is incomprehensible yet inspirational, bringing hope and assurance.

The older I get, the more I ponder the resurrection and the more I wonder about the nature of life in the new heaven and the new earth (Revelation 21). Many questions remain:

- Will the body of a premature baby or an amputee or an elderly person or a person confined to a wheelchair on earth be transformed in heaven into the body of a strong, agile, wrinkle-free young adult in prime physical condition?

- Will we be driving some kind of extraterrestrial vehicles, or will we simply blink an eye and be transported effortlessly and quickly to a new destination?

- Will animals be living among us?

- Will my favorite foods (medium-rare rib eye steak, marinated pork tenderloin, grilled chicken drumsticks/thighs, and lightly grilled salmon) be available? (See Luke 24:42–43.)

- Will my least favorite foods (brussels sprouts, yellow squash, okra, cilantro, peppers, and onions) be nowhere to be found? (See Genesis 3:17–18.)

The resurrection of the body and life everlasting are made possible by the price Jesus paid during the days in His life we now observe as Holy Week. In that new life, believers in Christ will be in His presence eternally. "And God will wipe away every tear from their eyes" (Revelation 7:17).

That's a promise worthy of joyful anticipation! Have a blessed Festival of the Resurrection!

Outward Appearance

VOLUME VII, NUMBER 40—APRIL 28, 2016

This past Sunday, I had the privilege of teaching Bible class at our congregation, Zion Lutheran Church in Walburg, Texas. The topic was the selection of a successor to King Saul, the man chosen to be the first king of the people of Israel. The title of the topic was "From Shepherd to King."

King Saul was on his way out when the prophet Samuel was told by God to go to the house of a man named Jesse, where he would find the man God had selected to be Saul's replacement. One by one, Jesse's sons were paraded before Samuel, who chose each of the first two fairly quickly. Each was a man of stature and made a very favorable impression. Both were nixed by the Almighty. So were all the rest of the sons of Jesse who were paraded before Samuel.

When Samuel asked if there were any more sons, Jesse said there was one more, a young man out in the fields taking care of the sheep. Samuel asked Jesse to bring in that final son, described in the Bible as ruddy and handsome, with beautiful eyes. Immediately, the Lord told Samuel to anoint this sixteen-year-old named David to be the next king of Israel.

The most significant factor in this selection process was the Lord's direction to Samuel: "Do not look on his appearance or on the height of his stature. . . . For the LORD sees not as man sees: man looks on the outward appearance, but the LORD looks on the heart" (1 Samuel 16:7).

During the class, I shared a number of details about the life of David before he was actually inaugurated as king, including his miraculous defeat of the Philistine giant Goliath, nine and a half feet tall. Then I shared the story of Susan Boyle, 2009 contestant on *Britain's Got Talent*.

Hardly the fairest lady in the land, Susan did not impress program hosts and judges Piers Morgan, Amanda Holden, and Simon Cowell. Even people in the audience were aghast at her very lackluster, homely appearance. However, after the first few notes of a powerful song from *Les Misérables* came out of her mouth, opinions changed drastically and visibly.

The YouTube video I played for the class showed the incredulous looks on the faces of the judges and audience members when the end of her song was greeted with an enthusiastic, elongated standing ovation. All three judges offered superlative evaluations of her performance!

Susan Boyle was a phenomenal personification of the truth of what God told the prophet Samuel hundreds of years ago: people look at outward appearance. The Lord looks at the heart!

God anointed lowly David and used him to point many people to the Messiah! David became an ancestor of Christ! God created each of us and gave us special gifts. Regardless of your outward appearance, the Lord looks at your heart. What great things does God have in store for you?

Trusting God's Promise

VOLUME VII, NUMBER 44—MAY 26, 2016

This article is intended specifically for Terry's and my fellow members at Zion Lutheran Church in Walburg, Texas. It's also directed toward every person, young or old, lay or clergy, faced with the decision of how much is enough to give back to God. That's not always a simple decision.

A couple months ago it became obvious that the total weekly offerings at Zion were falling about 20 percent short of the amount required to meet budgeted expenses. On several separate occasions, I expressed to Terry my concern about this matter. A few weeks later, we decided to do something.

Our decision was to increase the amount of our weekly offering by 25 percent. Frankly, this was not an easy decision. Last year, we had pledged a sizable amount for Zion's three-year capital stewardship campaign. Already stretching our finances to meet that challenging pledge, the thought of adding an additional 25 percent to our weekly offering caused me to furrow my brow.

Then I read again the words of Malachi 3. God said to the people of Israel, "You are robbing Me" (v. 8a). The people asked, "How have we robbed You?" (v. 8b). God answered, "In your tithes and contributions. You are cursed with a curse, for you are robbing Me, the whole nation of you. Bring the full tithe into the storehouse, that there may be food in My house. And thereby put Me to the test, says the LORD of hosts, if I will not open the windows of heaven for you and pour down for you a blessing until there is no more need" (vv. 8b–10).

Really not anticipating any specific blessings over and above the spiritual ones we've been receiving bountifully throughout the fifty years of our lives together, imagine our surprise when two totally unexpected checks arrived in the mail within weeks of our decision to increase our weekly tithe and offering! The sum of those checks was over five times more than the total amount by which our offerings were increased for an entire year!

This past Sunday afternoon I shared this story with the crowd of folks who had gathered for our congregational voters meeting for the purpose of adopting our budget for the coming fiscal year. It was not an easy meeting. I expressed to the crowd my wonderment whether those two checks would have arrived even if we had not made the decision to increase our weekly offerings. I quickly added that although that may certainly have been the case, I would always be convinced that they came in fulfillment of God's promise in Malachi 3.

My encouragement to each of you, dear friends in Christ, is to put the Lord to the test, as He has challenged us to do. The bountiful blessings you receive may not be the same as ours. They may be even greater! Regardless of the type or amount of your blessings, I pray and predict that you will experience special joy in the process of anticipating the fulfillment of God's promise!

Memorial Day Legacy

VOLUME VII, NUMBER 45—JUNE 2, 2016

This past Monday, our nation celebrated Memorial Day. It's a day to remember and to give thanks to God for the women and men who gave their lives while serving in our country's armed forces and those who are still living today. If you are a veteran or are related to a veteran, especially one who died while in the armed services, please accept my sincere appreciation and that of a grateful nation for your or your loved one's faithful and self-sacrificing service.

Last Friday's *USA Today* in a table titled "The Toll of War" listed the number of US deaths in major wars of the past 250 years. Information came from the Congressional Research Service and US Defense Department. Here's the list:

Revolutionary War	4,435
War of 1812	2,260
Mexican War	13,283
Civil War	625,000
Spanish-American War	2,446
World War I	116,516
World War II	405,399
Korean War	36,574
Vietnam War	58,220
Persian Gulf War	383
Afghanistan War	2,349
Iraq War	4,424
Total	1,271,289

Those who have served in the military, whether or not that service required the ultimate sacrifice of life itself, have created a legacy. That's a word that means "gift, bequest, inheritance, heritage, contribution." The gift given by those we honor each Memorial Day is that of defending and protecting our country's freedoms and the safety of its citizens. Beyond that is the gift to their living family members of the godly example of honor, valor, courage, humility, and commitment.

First Peter 4:10–11 reminds us: "As each has received a gift, use it to serve one another, as good stewards of God's varied grace: whoever speaks, as one who speaks oracles of God; whoever serves, as one who serves by the strength that God supplies—in order that in everything God may be glorified through Jesus Christ. To Him belong glory and dominion forever and ever. Amen."

Jesus said: "Greater love has no one than this, that someone lay down his life for his friends" (John 15:13).

Thank God for those who have served and continue to serve in our nation's armed forces!

Diversity and Direction in America

VOLUME VIII, NUMBER 2—AUGUST 4, 2016

Only someone living in a cave could plead ignorance about the diversity that exists in our country and the decision ahead about the direction in which we'll be going. The Republican and Democratic conventions held last month made it quite clear that our two political parties hold significantly different opinions on many important matters and diametrically opposite positions on others.

Issues at hand include abortion, national security, terrorism in the world, racial tensions in America, the national debt, the Affordable Care Act, gun control, support for military veterans, and Supreme Court appointments. We could add to the list.

Just over three months from now, America will choose a new leader. Wouldn't it be great if at least one nominee for president would actually approach all or even most of these matters the way many of us would like? While that's not likely to happen, many voters have already decided which candidate would be the best leader for America's future. Others are still pondering. Many Americans are frustrated and disenchanted with the options. Quite a few believe more qualified candidates should have arisen. Be that as it may, the choice is before us.

It may help to remember, though not always easy to accept, "There is no authority except from God, and those [governing authorities] that exist have been instituted by God" (Romans 13:1). God acts through humans. Our next president will be elected by American voters through the 538 members of the electoral college, not directly appointed or anointed by God. Exercise your constitutional right to vote. Not to vote for any candidate is to yield the election to those who do.

For now, join me in prayer that God will use this election to accomplish His will for our lives.

Worth Remembering

VOLUME VIII, NUMBER 3—AUGUST 11, 2016

Last week Terry shared with me a story she had received via email; the author is unknown. An elderly man whose wife had recently died attended his seventy-fifth high school reunion. Soon after arriving, he saw across the room an old high school girlfriend whose husband had also passed away. He immediately went across the room, engaged in conversation with her, and asked her to dance.

The couple spent the entire evening on the dance floor. As the reunion party ended, the man asked his old flame if she would marry him. She quickly replied, "Yes!" The two ninety-three-year-olds kissed excitedly, exchanged phone numbers, and parted company for the night.

The next morning the man, whose memory wasn't what it used to be, remembered having a great evening. But he couldn't recall for certain whether he had actually asked his high school sweetheart to marry him. So he picked up the phone and called her to find out.

When she answered the phone, he asked: "Did I ask you to marry me last night?" Her ecstatic reply was: "Thank you so much for calling! I remembered receiving a marriage proposal, but I couldn't remember from whom it came!"

Next Monday will be the fifty-first anniversary of the night I asked my dear Terry to marry me. I recall it clearly. For fifty-one years I've had no trouble remembering the significance of August 15, 1965!

Neither of us has been out of high school seventy-five years. Yet both of us sometimes have minor lapses of memory, finding it occasionally difficult to recall what so far have been matters of minor significance. Perhaps you can identify with that reality.

Some things are never forgotten. Births, Baptisms, confirmations, parents, siblings, grandparents, friends, teachers, pastors, educational experiences, marriages, children, vocational callings, grandchildren, and deaths of family members and personal friends. Many of these are likely on your lists of people, events, and experiences worth remembering.

One more thing worth remembering: "It is the LORD who goes before you. He will be with you; He will not leave you or forsake you. Do not fear or be dismayed" (Deuteronomy 31:8).

Thank God for experiences and people of significance in your life! And thank God for His grace! That's a blessing absolutely worth remembering!

Important People in Your Life

Volume VIII, Number 5—August 25, 2016

The following quiz about important people is often attributed to Charles Schulz, creator of the *Peanuts* comic strip. That attribution is denied by Snopes .com, a widely used internet reliability resource. Nevertheless, its point is worthy of consideration. So here it is, slightly amended:

1. Name the five wealthiest people in the world.
2. Name the last five Heisman trophy winners.
3. Name the last five winners of the Miss America pageant.
4. Name ten people who have won the Nobel or Pulitzer Prize.
5. Name the last half dozen Academy Award winners for best actor and actress.
6. Name the last decade's World Series winners.

How did you do? If you're like me, you didn't do so well. The point of this little exercise is that very few people remember the headliners of yesterday. These are not second-rate achievers. They are the best in their fields.

But the applause dies. Awards tarnish. Achievements are forgotten. Except in rare cases, accolades, certificates, and trophies are buried with their owners. I look around my office at many such items that will very likely find their permanent home someday in a dumpster.

Here's another quiz. See how you do on this one:

1. List a few teachers who aided your journey through school.
2. Name three friends who helped you through a difficult time.
3. Name five people who taught you something worthwhile.
4. Think of a few people who made you feel appreciated and special.
5. Think of five people you enjoy spending time with.
6. Name the pastor who most significantly influenced your life.

For many people, this second quiz is easier than the first. That's true simply because the people who make a difference in our lives are not the ones who possess impressive credentials, high net worth, or prestigious awards. They simply are the people who care the most.

Scripture has many injunctions to honor important people, including those in authority (Romans 13:7), your leaders in the Lord's work (1 Thessalonians 5:12), your father and your mother (Deuteronomy 5:16).

Take some time to honor the important people in your life!

Lest We Forget

VOLUME VIII, NUMBER 7—SEPTEMBER 8, 2016

Fifteen years ago this coming Sunday, life changed in America and around the world. Most of us vividly remember that day, September 11, 2001, now known worldwide as 9/11. Images of the twin towers of the World Trade Center in New York City burning and collapsing are indelibly etched in our minds and hearts.

In a meeting of the Council of Presidents of The Lutheran Church—Missouri Synod on September 25, 2001, leaders of our church body reached out to the nation by drafting and unanimously approving a full-page statement published October 2, 2001, in *USA Today* and the *New York Times*. Here's the text of that statement, titled "A Promise":

A PROMISE

In the aftermath of our nation's tragedy three weeks ago today, we of The Lutheran Church—Missouri Synod wholeheartedly offer our love and prayers for those tens of thousands of people whose lives have been drastically altered by the sudden loss of their loved ones and friends. At such a time it is natural to wonder how we can get on with life.

Still heavy with the burden of our enormous loss, we face the potential for even more danger at our doorstep. And as we look out upon the world seeking a promise of comfort and hope, we may see only darkness. Yet we are not the first people to suffer such darkness, nor to long for such a promise.

David in the Old Testament, in time of great personal and national distress, looked to God and took comfort in His promise: "The Lord is my shepherd. . . . Even though I walk through the valley of the shadow of death, I will fear no evil, for You are with me."

Jesus, to whom the Scriptures refer as our "Good Shepherd," spoke words that are particularly poignant right now: "Greater love has no one than this, that he lay down his life for his friends."

That Good Shepherd understands suffering and death . . . and His own death and resurrection promise hope and comfort to us all.

In these days of great personal and national trial, it is important to remember the words of St. Paul as we struggle with "getting on with life": "For I am convinced that neither death nor life, neither angels nor demons, neither the present nor the future, nor any powers, neither height nor depth, nor anything else in all creation, will be able to separate us from the love of God that is in Christ Jesus our Lord."

And that's His promise!

If you were alive September 11, 2001, and old enough that day to grasp the gravity of what occurred, you will always remember 9/11. And so will I, remembering God's promise that nothing will be able to separate us from the love of God that is in Christ Jesus our Lord!

The Virtue of Humility

VOLUME VIII, NUMBER 12—OCTOBER 13, 2016

On more than one occasion, I've meet and spoken with people who say they used to attend church, but don't anymore. I'm always saddened when I come away from that kind of conversation.

Sometimes human pride erects unnecessary barriers that contribute to a person's departure from God's Word and Sacraments. Here's a story by an unknown author that illustrates this truth:

One Sunday morning, an old cowboy entered a church just before worship time. Although the old man and his clothes were spotlessly clean, he wore jeans, a denim shirt, and boots that were ragged and worn. In his hand he carried a worn-out hat and an equally worn out Bible.

The church he entered was in a very upscale and exclusive part of the city. It was the largest and most beautiful church the old cowboy had ever seen. The people of the congregation were all dressed in expensive clothes and accessories. As the cowboy took a seat, the others moved away from him. No one greeted, spoke to, or welcomed him. They were all appalled at his appearance and did not attempt to hide it.

As the old cowboy was leaving the church, the preacher approached him and asked the cowboy to do him a favor. "Before you come back in here again, have a talk with God and ask Him what He thinks would be appropriate attire for worship." The old cowboy assured the preacher he would.

The next Sunday, he showed back up for the services wearing the same ragged jeans, shirt, boots, and hat. Once again he was completely shunned. The preacher approached the man and said, "I thought I asked you to speak to God before you came back to our church".

"I did," replied the old cowboy.

"What did God tell you the proper attire should be for worshiping here?" asked the preacher.

"Well, sir, God told me that He didn't have a clue what I should wear. He said He'd never been in this church."

While unable to vouch for the veracity of this story, I believe it illustrates what Jesus had in mind when He told the story of the Pharisee and the tax collector in the temple. The Pharisee said: "God, I thank You that I am not like other men, extortioners, unjust, adulterers, or even like this tax collector. I fast twice a week; I give tithes of all that I get" (Luke 18:11–12). The tax collector prayed: "God, be merciful to me, a sinner!" (v. 13).

Jesus concluded the story, "Everyone who exalts himself will be humbled, but the one who humbles himself will be exalted" (v. 14). As we remember and live those words, people who visit our church, even in blue jeans, will find love and acceptance from God and from His people!

Obstacles in Life

VOLUME VIII, NUMBER 19—DECEMBER 1, 2016

A story, from an unknown author, that can be found widely online: One day a man walking down a path saw a butterfly cocoon that was about to open. As he watched, a small opening appeared in the cocoon. For several hours, the butterfly struggled to force its body through that little hole. Then it seemed to stop making any progress. It appeared to have gone as far as it could go.

So the man decided to help the butterfly. He took a pair of scissors and opened the cocoon. The butterfly emerged easily, but it had a withered body. It was tiny and its wings were shriveled.

The man continued to watch because he expected that at any moment the wings would open, enlarge, and expand, to be able to support the butterfly's body. That didn't happen. In fact, the butterfly spent the rest of its life crawling around with a withered body and shriveled wings. It never was able to take flight.

What the man in his kindness and good intentions did not understand was that the restricting cocoon and the struggle required for the butterfly to get through the tiny opening were nature's way of forcing fluid from the body of the butterfly into its wings so that it would be ready for flight once it achieved freedom from the cocoon.

Sometimes struggles are exactly what we need in our life. If allowed to go through life without any obstacles, we would not be as strong as we might otherwise have been. Essentially, without struggles or obstacles we might never be able to achieve what God created us to accomplish.

One writer's applications of this story to life:

I asked for strength and was given difficulties to make me strong.
I asked for prosperity and was given a brain and brawn to work.
I asked for courage and was given obstacles to overcome.
I asked for love and was given troubled people to help.
I asked for wisdom and was given problems to solve.

I asked for favors and was given opportunities.
I received nothing I wanted but everything I needed.

The moral of this story: Live life without fear and confront obstacles that arise, knowing and trusting that by God's grace and with His power, "nothing will be impossible" (Luke 1:37)!

"Only God Can Do This!"

VOLUME VIII, NUMBER 25—JANUARY 12, 2017

A January 10 article by Dr. Jim Denison: "What Impressed Me Even More Than Clemson's Win" (https://www.denisonforum.org/columns/cultural-commentary/impressed-even-clemsons-win/):

> *In what's being called "the best title game in college football history," the Clemson Tigers defeated the Alabama Crimson Tide last night on a touchdown with one second left in the game. It was one of the greatest games I've ever seen and Clemson's first victory over Alabama since 1905.*
>
> *For years to come, Clemson fans will be discussing the feats of quarterback Deshaun Watson and diminutive wide receiver Hunter Renfrow, who caught the game-winner. Freshman quarterback Jalen Hurts nearly won the game for Alabama before Clemson's last-minute heroics.*
>
> *As great as the players were, the coaches impressed me even more.*
>
> *Clemson's head coach was born William Christopher Swinney. His older brother Tripp started calling him "That Boy," which became "Dabo," the name by which he has been known his entire life.*
>
> *His childhood was more than challenging—his father became an alcoholic; his oldest brother was severely injured in a car accident and has battled alcoholism for much of his life. His parents eventually divorced, and he lived with his mother in a series of motels, apartments, and friends' homes. Swinney was nonetheless an honor roll student and football star in high school.*
>
> *He enrolled in Alabama in 1988 and eventually won a scholarship on the football team. His mother, who had recovered from debilitating polio (including an iron lung and fourteen months in a knee-to-neck cast), shared an apartment room with him while he was in college. He earned a bachelor's degree and MBA at Alabama and eventually made his way*

to Clemson, where he has been head coach since 2008. Swinney became a Christian at a Fellowship of Christian Athletes meeting. He is so public about his faith in Christ that the Freedom From Religion Foundation threatened to sue him and Clemson, but they could not find a player willing to file a complaint against the coach.

Alabama's legendary coach Nick Saban is also a strong Christian. He attends Mass before football games and is a regular at his parish church in Tuscaloosa, Alabama. He and his wife are founders of the foundation Nick's Kids, which has raised more than $6 million to help children in need. Last year, they built their sixteenth Habitat for Humanity house to honor Alabama's sixteenth national title in the school's history.

Both coaches say that winning titles is important, but what matters most are the young people they coach. One of Saban's players said of him, "He doesn't get enough credit for teaching guys how to become men." When players from Saban's ten seasons at Alabama gathered last year, one of them spoke for all: "Coach, you changed everybody's life, no matter if you knew it or not."

Similarly, Swinney says, "My driving force in this business is to create and build great men." The most rewarding experiences of coaching, he says, have come when former players tell him he made a positive impact on their lives.

In our scientific age, it's hard to value intangible souls more than tangible success. But of all God created in the entire universe, human beings are the only creation he made in his own image (Genesis 1:26–27). Investing in people is clearly your best way to leave your mark on eternity.

According to national champion coach Dabo Swinney, "The value of life is measured in relationships, not results or riches."

I wholeheartedly agree and am thankful that men such as the coaches in this article are spending their lives and dedicating their careers to the development of leaders based on more than simply fame and fortune. May their number increase!

At the conclusion of Monday night's national title game, Clemson coach Dabo Swinney said: "Only God can do this!" While I'm not convinced that the God of the universe really cares about which football team wins the national championship, I'm thankful for Coach Swinney's public testimony of faith, giving credit and thanks to God for this significant achievement.

Harvey

VOLUME IX, NUMBER 6—AUGUST 31, 2017

Growing up, I never knew a person named Harvey. I only knew that name as the title of a 1950 movie. Harvey was Jimmy Stewart's invisible friend, a 6′3″ rabbit.

As a result of the past several days, the name Harvey will go down in American history not as an imaginary four-legged friend but as a horrible hurricane that left in its wake untold destruction and devastation. It first came ashore Saturday, August 26, in Rockport, Texas, as a category four hurricane. Eventually, it lost wind velocity and was redesignated as a category one hurricane and then a tropical storm.

Winds gusting up to 130 mph wreaked huge damage on several coastal cities. Homes, hotels, buildings, businesses, vehicles, and boats were damaged and destroyed.

Harvey eventually moved north and east along the Gulf Coast. It impacted 350 miles of coastline from Texas to Louisiana, including Galveston, Houston, Beaumont, Port Arthur, and many smaller outlying communities, leaving up to sixty inches of torrential flood-producing rainfall in its path.

Harvey's economic impact is huge. Hundreds of thousands have widespread damage to their homes and possessions, many with no flood insurance. They are left to pick up the pieces of their lives.

Relatively few people appear to have lost their lives in this historic storm. That's miraculous, considering the fact that millions of people live in Harvey's path of thousands of miles.

Ironically, this past Tuesday marked the twelfth anniversary of Hurricane Katrina, which in 2005 affected the Gulf Coast from central Florida to eastern Texas, especially devastating New Orleans and Mississippi coastal towns. For many, Harvey is a reminder of past tragedy and trauma.

Although devastating natural disasters like Harvey raise lots of questions in my mind about the will of God, here are a few thoughts and observations, some original, some borrowed, some inspired:

- People from across the country came to Texas to help, bringing together, face-to-face, women and men of differing race, nationality, and religious preference. Individuals and corporations pitched in, offering financial and in-kind resources where needed.

- Providing such care and life-saving assistance makes me believe that America is not what happened in Charlottesville. America is what is happening in Houston and beyond.

- Following the Old Testament flood, God provided a rainbow as a promise that never again would He send a flood to destroy the earth or all living creatures. (See Genesis 9:11.)

- In Old Testament prophet Elijah's presence, the Lord was not in a wind, not in an earthquake, not in a fire, but in a still, small voice, a gentle whisper. (See 1 Kings 19:11–13.)

- Jesus calmed a storm on the Sea of Galilee with a word of rebuke. (See Matthew 8:26.)

God's promise: "Fear not, for I have redeemed you; I have called you by name, you are Mine. When you pass through the waters, I will be with you; and through the rivers, they shall not overwhelm you. . . . For I am the LORD your God, the Holy One of Israel, your Savior" (Isaiah 43:1–2, 3).

Stress in Life

Volume IX, Number 7—September 7, 2017

Most people have stress in life. It comes in all forms. It can be financial, relational, professional, familial, physical, emotional, or psychological.

Wouldn't it be great if stress were to be totally eliminated from life? That's not realistic. Stress is a reality. It's the result of sin. We all sin. We all experience stress. We can't get away from it. Even though stress is unavoidable and not enjoyable, under normal circumstances it can be manageable. Not all circumstances are normal. Some stressors are beyond our control.

Consider the stress experienced by victims of Hurricane Harvey. They were all just minding their own business of living and working, with normal levels of stress. Out of the blue, an unwelcome intruder entered their lives, bringing with it unimaginable destruction and devastation.

To the trouble and trauma of Harvey is added the pending presence of Irma, headed toward currently predicted landfall in the United States. Florida's governor has already declared an emergency in that highly vulnerable state.

Overshadowed by news about Harvey and Irma are dozens of wildfires in western states, occurring even now. Those states include Washington, Oregon, California, Idaho, and Montana.

On top of the stress that accompanies these natural disasters, consider the idiocy of the supreme leader of the Democratic People's Republic of Korea. North Korea's Kim Jong-un has ordered way-too-frequent tests of missiles and hydrogen bombs that pose a very real threat to the US. At least fourteen such missile launches have occurred since February of this year.

So we face normal stress of daily living, uninvited stress from natural disasters, and international stress from a rogue nation with a leader seemingly hell-bent on nuclear destruction. What are we to do? How are we to live? Where do we turn for comfort and assurance?

Try these words from Psalm 46:1–3, 6–7, 9, 10–11:

God is our refuge and strength,

a very present help in trouble.

Therefore we will not fear though the earth gives way,

though the mountains be moved into the heart of the sea,

though its waters roar and foam,

though the mountains tremble at its swelling. . . .

The nations rage, the kingdoms totter;

He utters His voice, the earth melts.

The Lord of hosts is with us;

the God of Jacob is our fortress. . . .

He makes wars cease to the end of the earth. . . .

"Be still, and know that I am God.

I will be exalted among the nations,

I will be exalted in the earth!"

The Lord of hosts is with us;

the God of Jacob is our fortress.

Why Do People Rebuild after a Disaster?

Volume IX, Number 8—September 14, 2017

This past Monday, we were reminded of the traumatic events of an unforgettable day—September 11, 2001. We saw images of destruction, but we also saw photos of a new tower and a strikingly powerful memorial in New York City. After that disaster, rebuilding occurred.

Earlier this week I read an article by Rev. Bob Tasler (www.bobtasler.com), retired LCMS pastor living in Colorado. Much of his article is shared here with his permission.

In a Denver Post *article Greg Dobbs asked: "Why do people rebuild after a disaster?" Hurricanes destroy homes, wildfires burn businesses, and floods ruin communities. But when you ask disaster survivors what they plan to do, nearly all will say, "We will rebuild again."*

Why? Knowing another hurricane or wildfire or flood might come again, why do people continue to build in places that are prone to such disasters?

Dobbs asked a man who had lost homes in three hurricanes why he planned to rebuild again.

Instead of giving him reasons, the man asked, "Where are you from?" "Originally San Francisco," Dobbs said. "Don't they have earthquakes there?" "Yes, but I live in Colorado now," Dobbs said. "Don't y'all have wild fires in Colorado?" said the man. Yes, Dobbs told him, in 2012 and 2013 Colorado lost over a thousand homes to forest fires, and most of them rebuilt their homes again.

Communities along the Mississippi are destroyed by floods, but they rebuild again. People from Oklahoma and Kansas see homes and towns torn apart by tornadoes, but they, too, rebuild. Colorado has had enormous hailstorms destroy homes, autos, and buildings, but people still rebuild. Dobbs concluded his article, "If one doesn't get you, another might."

Why do we rebuild in those places again? My dad once told me, "Everyone has to be somewhere." So simple, yet so true. With seven billion people on our planet, everyone has to be somewhere, and there is no place without some danger.

I've got some bad news: Humans are responsible for all these disasters. Yup, it's all our fault, but not for the reasons climate alarmists would have us believe.

The original perfection of our world has been messed up by sin. Genesis 3 tells us God cursed the ground because of mankind's rebellion. Because of our sin, individually and corporately, we people have pain and suffering, no matter where we live. Thorns and thistles, work and sweat, pain of childbirth and families, all will be the lot of mankind until we return to the dust from which we were taken. That's the reason for the disasters, not plastic or coal or carbon dioxide.

But there is good news. God has promised us not only forgiveness, but also a new heaven and a new earth in the future, where "God's dwelling place is now among the people, and He will dwell with them. They will be His people, and God Himself will be with them and be their God. He will wipe every tear from their eyes. There will be no more death or mourning or crying or pain, for the old order of things has passed away" (Revelation 21:3–4 NIV).

Meanwhile, we live and rebuild and do our best to find joy in the life God has given us. The new heavens and new earth will come because of God's goodness in Jesus Christ. He will one day give His followers a more perfect existence. I look forward to that day with great hope!

May God protect and defend all who face disaster, and bring them new life and hope!

Onward, Christian Soldiers

VOLUME IX, NUMBER 13—OCTOBER 19, 2017

One of my favorite ancient childhood memories is a privilege that was afforded each child in Sunday School at St. Matthew Lutheran Church in Houston. All children and teachers gathered in the auditorium for a joint opening with hymn and prayer before going to our individual classes.

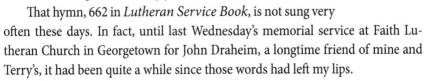

During that brief time the week before a child's birthday, he or she was invited to pick the hymn for that day. My favorite was "Onward, Christian Soldiers." I picked it every year.

That hymn, 662 in *Lutheran Service Book*, is not sung very often these days. In fact, until last Wednesday's memorial service at Faith Lutheran Church in Georgetown for John Draheim, a longtime friend of mine and Terry's, it had been quite a while since those words had left my lips.

Stanza 2 goes like this:

Like a mighty army
Moves the Church of God;
Brothers, we are treading
Where the saints have trod.
We are not divided,
All one body we,
One in hope and doctrine,
One in charity.
Onward, Christian soldiers,
Marching as to war,
With the cross of Jesus
Going on before.

As I sang that verse last week, my mind wandered to the question of whether the Church of God was or was not more united in hope, in doctrine, and in charity than it is today. We know from history that the Church has often had struggles and divisions and most likely always will have.

What gives me hope are the words of stanza 3:

Crowns and thrones may perish,
Kingdoms rise and wane,
But the Church of Jesus
Constant will remain.
Gates of hell can never
'Gainst that Church prevail;
We have Christ's own promise,
And that cannot fail.
Onward, Christian soldiers,
Marching as to war,
With the cross of Jesus
Going on before.

That's still one of my favorite hymns!

A Thanksgiving Dream

VOLUME IX, NUMBER 18—NOVEMBER 21, 2017

Recently I read a story from an unknown author about a man who dreamed he went to heaven. When he arrived, an angel began showing him around. Here's the story:

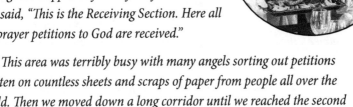

The angel and I walked side-by-side inside a large workroom filled with other angels. My angel guide stopped in front of the first section and said, "This is the Receiving Section. Here all the prayer petitions to God are received."

This area was terribly busy with many angels sorting out petitions written on countless sheets and scraps of paper from people all over the world. Then we moved down a long corridor until we reached the second section.

The angel said, "This is the Packaging and Delivery Section. Here all the blessings people asked for are processed and delivered to those who requested them."

I noticed again how busy that area was. There were lots of angels working hard at that station. Many blessings had been requested and were being packaged for delivery to Earth.

Finally, at the farthest end of the long corridor we stopped at the door of a very small station. To my great surprise, only one angel was seated there, idly doing nothing. "This is the Acknowledgment Section," my angel friend quietly admitted to me. He seemed embarrassed.

"How is it that there is no work going on here?" I asked.

"So sad," the angel sighed. "After people receive the blessings they asked for, very few respond with acknowledgments."

"How does one acknowledge God's blessings?" I asked.

"*Simple,*" the angel answered. Just say, "*Thank You, God.*"

"*What blessings should they acknowledge?*" I asked.

The angel replied: "If you have food in the refrigerator, clothes on your back, a roof overhead, and a place to sleep, you are richer than 75 percent of the people in this world.

"*If you have money in the bank, in your wallet, and spare change in a dish, you are among the top 8 percent of the world's wealthy.*

"*If you received this message on your own computer, you are part of the 1 percent in the world who have that opportunity.*

"*If you woke up this morning with more health than illness, you are more blessed than the many who will not even survive this day.*

"*If you have never experienced the fear of battle, the loneliness of imprisonment, the agony of torture, or the pangs of starvation, you are ahead of 700 million people in the world.*

"*If you can attend a church without the fear of any harassment, arrest, torture, or death, you are envied by and more blessed than three billion people in the world.*

"*If you can hold your head up high and smile, you are quite different from all those in the world who live in doubt and despair.*

"*If you can read this message, you are more blessed than billions of people in the world who cannot read at all.*"

Motivated to action, I said, "What now? How can I start?"

The angel said, "Bow your head right now and thank God for His bountiful blessings!"

Happy Thanksgiving! Have a good day, count your blessings, and pray with me:

Thank You, Lord, for the many blessings I have received and continue to receive every day. Help me never forget the source of these blessings and always to remember to praise You for all Your goodness in my life. Help me do so every day, until the day that, with all Your saints, I will praise You eternally in Your heavenly kingdom; through Jesus Christ my Lord. Amen.

A Clean Windshield

VOLUME IX, NUMBER 19—NOVEMBER 30, 2017

As long as I've been driving, I've been pretty much a fanatic about keeping my car clean.

My current car is silver in color. Thankfully, that color does not easily show road grime, dust, and dirt. As a matter of fact, the primary clue that it's time to wash is a dirty windshield. I can't stand a dirty windshield! It bugs me to have a dirty windshield! Pardon the pun.

So one option is to pull into a service station that appears to have decently clean windshield washing solution, a squeegee that's new enough not to leave streaks, and paper towels to enhance the process. Finding a station that meets those three criteria is not an easy task.

If my schedule allows, I'll usually skip that process and go straight to the car wash. I have a special deal at a local establishment that allows unlimited exterior washes for a reasonable fixed price. Terry can also wash her car for a slightly lower monthly fee. Such a deal!

One would think a freshly washed car would have a nice, clean windshield. Not so. The dudes at the car wash don't seem to understand how important a clean windshield is to fanatics like me. So they wipe the windows with a grimy rag that leaves unacceptable streaks on the windshield.

Alas! What to do? Quit this place and find a new one? Not so easy. In addition to being a clean windshield fanatic, I'm also quite frugal. The price at other car wash establishments in our town is ridiculously ridiculous! So I suffer through streaky windshields and the frustration they bring.

Sort of reminds me of St. Paul's words about present and future reality in 1 Corinthians 13:12: "For now we see in a mirror [or window!] dimly, but then face to face. Now I know in part; then I shall know fully, even as I have been fully known."

I feel Paul's pain every time I get behind a dirty windshield.

But then he writes these more familiar words of greater significance: "So now faith, hope, and love abide, these three; but the greatest of these is love" (13:13).

I love a clean car and a spotless windshield. But that love fades into an insignificant speck on the window of life when compared to the love of God for us and the love we express to Him in return.

Think about that love as the season of Advent arrives this Sunday. It marks the beginning of our spiritual preparation for the celebration of the birth of Jesus. A blessed Advent to you!

Jesus Loves the Little Children

Volume IX, Number 21—December 14, 2017

That was the topic of my brief devotion at the office of the Texas District of The Lutheran Church—Missouri Synod this week. I shared some graphic representations of little children with Jesus and three actual photos of God's children living today.

Photo 1 was my grandniece Amanda Wheaton and her two children, Emma Grace and Anna Christine. Some of you may recall that they are the survivors of triplets born prematurely (about one pound six ounces each) on Christmas Day 2013. That means they will turn four years old this Christmas. Their little brother, Logan Christopher, met Jesus the day after he was born.

Although not without ongoing physical challenges, Emma and Anna are doing remarkably well, by the grace of God. Jesus loves Emma and Anna. And Jesus also loves Logan.

Photo 2 was fifteen-month-old Lily Grace Stigall, great-granddaughter of Marlene Hahn, who worked for many years in the Texas District LCMS office. Lily is in Dell Children's Hospital in Austin after a Thanksgiving evening fall into a backyard pool. Initially fighting for her life, Lily is now breathing on her own, yet faces many challenges on the road to restoration.

Thousands of people across the nation and around the world are praying for her complete recovery, which would be truly miraculous. Please join Lily's parents, grandparents, great-grandparents, and their entire family in praying for this precious child. Jesus loves Lily.

Photo 3 was my 101⅔-year-old mother, Elda Kieschnick. Although in a much different chronological category than Emma, Anna, and Lily, Mother Elda is still very much a child of God, who prays every day to see Him face-to-face. Jesus loves Elda.

That's the message of Christmas, my dear friends. Jesus loves the little children, no matter how old we are. Here's how the familiar song goes:

Jesus loves the little children, All the children of the world.
Ev'ry child in ev'ry land, Jesus holds them in His hand.
Jesus loves the little children of the world.

That includes you, my friend. God bless your day!

And Then It Is Winter

VOLUME IX, NUMBER 23—DECEMBER 28, 2017

For this final article in the Year of our Lord 2017, I'm sharing with you a story I've had in my files for some time, author unknown, slightly revised by yours truly:

Time has a way of moving quickly and catching us unaware of the passing years. It seems just yesterday that I was young, newly married, and embarking on my new life with my new spouse. Yet here it is, the winter of my life. How did I get here so fast? Where did all those years go?

Through the years I remember seeing older people and thinking they were years away from me. The winter of my life was so far off I could not fathom it or imagine what it would be like.

But here it is. My friends are retired and getting gray. Many of them move slowly. Some are in good shape, others not so much. Like me, their age is beginning to show. I am now those older folks I used to see but never thought I'd actually be.

Taking a nap is not a treat anymore, it's mandatory! If I don't take one on my own, I just fall asleep where I sit!

So now I enter this new season of my life unprepared for all the aches and pains and loss of strength and ability to go and do things I wish I had done but never did!

At least I know that though the winter has come, and I'm not sure how long it will last, when it's over on this earth, it's NOT over. A new adventure will begin! The Bible calls it heaven!

If you're not in your winter yet, let me remind you that it will be here faster than you think. So, whatever you would like to accomplish in your life, do it quickly! Don't put it off too long!

We have no promise that we will see all the seasons of our life. So live for today. Say all the things you want your loved ones to remember about your love for them, about God's love for them, and about all the things you have done with them in the years that passed so quickly!

Thus ends the story. Although I'm in the winter of my life chronologically, I feel like it's actually still the fall. Good health is a gift of God that is often taken for granted until it's gone.

Life is God's gift to you. The way you live your life is your gift to Him and to those who come after you. It is faith and health that are real wealth and not pieces of gold and silver. Today is the oldest you have ever been, yet the youngest you will ever be. So enjoy this day God has given you.

In whatever season of your life you happen to be living at this moment, Terry and I extend to you the assurance of our prayers for a blessed, healthy, and happy New Year!

The Power of Prayer

VOLUME IX, NUMBER 25—JANUARY 11, 2018

Before reading the story below, I had never heard of Pahrump, Nevada. Google it, and you'll see a listing of "adult entertainment" that gives an indication of what might be its "claim to fame."

Here's the story, from an unknown author:

In Pahrump, Nevada, the Diamond D brothel began construction on an expansion of their building to increase their ever-growing business.

In response, the local Baptist church started a campaign to block the business from expanding, with morning, afternoon, and evening prayer sessions at their church.

Work on Diamond D's project progressed until the week before the grand reopening when lightning struck the building and burned it to the ground! After the brothel burned to the ground by the lightning strike, the church folks were rather smug in their outlook, bragging about "the power of prayer."

But shortly thereafter, Jill Diamond, the owner/madam of Diamond D, sued the church, the preacher, and the entire congregation on the grounds that the church "was ultimately responsible for the demise of her building and her business, either through direct or indirect divine actions or means."

In its reply to the court, the church vehemently and vociferously denied any and all responsibility or any connection to the building's demise.

The crusty old judge read through the plaintiff's complaint and the defendant's reply, and at the opening hearing he commented, "I don't know how I'm going to decide this case, but it appears from the paperwork that we now have a brothel owner who staunchly believes in the power of prayer and an entire church congregation that thinks otherwise."

The moral of this story: we'd better be careful about how and for what we pray. If we really trust God to answer our prayer, when He answers the way we asked, we'd better be willing to say that that's exactly what happened and to give Him the credit.

Grief Is Love with No Place to Go

VOLUME IX, NUMBER 29—FEBRUARY 8, 2018

Yesterday would have been my mother and father's seventy-ninth wedding anniversary. They married on February 7, 1939, at Zion Lutheran Church in Alamo, Texas.

Dad went to heaven way too soon to suit Mom and the rest of our family. He was only sixty-six when he passed away New Year's Day 1983. He's been gone over thirty-five years.

Mother Elda, who might yet see her 102nd birthday on April 10, prays every day that she would be blessed by God to join Father Martin. But her desired answer has not yet been granted.

Elda misses Martin every day and longs to be reunited with him in heaven. The rest of our family, even those who were not yet born when he passed away but have only heard lots of stories about him, miss him also. Although it would be selfish for us not to affirm Mother's prayer that one day soon she'll wake up in heaven, we'll also truly miss her when she's gone.

In a very real sense, people who lose a loved one grieve that loss. It never really goes away.

The other day I read this definition of grief: "Grief, I've learned, is really just love. It's all the love you want to give but cannot. All of that unspent love gathers up in the corners of your eyes, the lump in your throat, and in that hollow part of your chest. Grief is just love with no place to go."

Over the years, our family has mostly learned to live with our grief. As the Third Article of the Apostles' Creed states, we believe "in the resurrection of the body, and the life everlasting."

That hope in our hearts keeps us from expressing grief by curling into a fetal position or doing a catatonic rock. We simply miss the man we called "Dad." He was a good man. Not perfect. But a dedicated Christian, hard-working provider, faithful husband, loving father and grandfather.

Most people I know can tell a similar story about grief for a loved one they've lost. That's likely true in your life as well. For me, some of the most consoling words in the Bible are 1 Thessalonians 4:13–14, 17–18:

> We do not want you to be uninformed, brothers, about those who are asleep, that you may not grieve as others do who have no hope. For since we believe that Jesus died and rose again, even so, through Jesus, God will bring with Him those who have fallen asleep. . . . And so we will always be with the Lord. Therefore encourage one another with these words.

Humanly speaking, grief is just love with no place to go. But we can do as the hymnwriter suggests:

> I lay my griefs on Jesus,
> My burdens and my cares;
> He from them all releases;
> He all my sorrows shares. (*LSB* 606:2)

From Weeping and Mourning to Joy and Hope

VOLUME IX, NUMBER 36—MARCH 28, 2018

As most Americans are aware, this is Holy Week. The days ahead include Maundy Thursday, Good Friday, Holy Saturday, and the Festival of the Resurrection of Our Lord, aka Easter.

Amid all the aspects of the secular observance of Easter, Christians focus on the resurrection of our Lord, Jesus Christ. It's an awesome story, recorded in the New Testament in Matthew 28, Mark 16, Luke 24, and John 20. I highly recommend you read all four accounts this week.

Lots of people will be in church this Sunday. Some are those lovingly referred to as CEO Christians: Christmas and Easter Only. Be that as it may, I hope and trust that pastors will focus not on the sporadic attendance of some but on the reality of death and our belief in "the resurrection of the body and the life everlasting" (Apostles' Creed, circa AD 390) by God's grace through Christ our Lord.

This statement of belief in the resurrection provides hope and comfort, especially at the time of death of loved ones and friends. Earlier this week I wrote a letter to a friend whose wife passed away suddenly last week. Here are some of the words I wrote:

> The author of Ecclesiastes writes: "For everything there is a season, . . . a time to be born, and a time to die; . . . a time to weep, and a time to laugh; a time to mourn, and a time to dance" (Ecclesiastes 3:1, 2, 4). The times of dying, weeping, and mourning are not happy times.
>
> That's true whether a loved one dies after a lengthy illness or with no advance warning. At a time like this we echo the words of Simon Peter to Jesus: "Lord, to whom shall we go? You have the words of eternal life" (John 6:68). That's where we go at a time like this. We go to Jesus.

Many years ago Jesus' loved ones went to His grave, grieving deeply. They had lost the one who had been expected to change the history of the whole world. But He had died, as all men do, and His was a bitter and painful death.

Yet as those mourners came, by a miracle of the grace and power of God, their grief was turned to joy, their despair to faith and confidence! Jesus had risen from the dead!

Ever since that first Easter morn, believing people have come to the grave of their loved ones in confidence and trust— weeping, mourning, but not despairing, not lost, awaiting the promised resurrection of their loved one and the new heaven and new earth that lie ahead (Revelation 21:1).

Terry and I pray that your times of weeping and mourning will be mitigated by the joy and hope that come from the peace of God that passes all understanding. We love you and thank God for you! A blessed Festival of the Resurrection! That's what I mean when I say: "Happy Easter!"

Not One Sparrow

VOLUME IX, NUMBER 44—MAY 24, 2018

Early one morning last week on the way to the office, I was traveling at forty-five mph on a two-lane road. All of a sudden, out of nowhere, two small birds flew from the grass and trees on my right, directly into my path. One flew at an altitude that allowed it to continue its flight. The other one flew directly into my right front fender and fell to the ground.

This was not the first time my vehicle had accidentally and unintentionally become an instrument that terminated the life of a living creature. Over my fifty-nine years of driving experience, I've hit other birds and a few squirrels. Transparency requires me to confess that willfully and intentionally I have also sent a few rattlesnakes to their eternal destiny. Scold me, if necessary.

The day of my encounter with the bird in question turned out to be the same day of yet another school shooting. This one was in Santa Fe. Not New Mexico. Texas. Frankly I don't recall ever knowing there was a Santa Fe in Texas. It's just a few miles south of Houston, my hometown. Sadly, Santa Fe is now known around the world as the site of a willful and intentional eruption of evil activity resulting in the death of eight students and two teachers.

As soon as the bird fell to the ground I remembered the words of Jesus: "Are not two sparrows sold for a penny? Yet not one of them will fall to the ground apart from your Father" (Matthew 10:29).

And when I heard the news that ten people had died that day, I immediately recalled more of Jesus' words in almost the same breath: "Do not fear those who kill the body but cannot kill the soul. Rather fear Him who can destroy both soul and body in hell" (Matthew 10:28).

But the words that have stuck with me even more poignantly are these: "Even the hairs of your head are all numbered. Fear not, therefore; you are of more value than many sparrows" (Matthew 10:30–31).

Is it possible to compare the life of a human with the life of a sparrow? No way. In God's eyes, all living creatures have value. But Jesus says the intrinsic value of human life far outweighs that of many sparrows.

That's why many more tears are shed when a human dies, regardless of the cause of death, than when a sparrow dies. Yet God's love is so magnificent that not one sparrow falls to the ground apart from the will of the Father.

CPSIA information can be obtained
at www.ICGtesting.com
Printed in the USA
LVHW04s2124250718
584935LV00002B/30/P